11/01

19.96

Princess Diana

Titles in the People in the News series include:

PEOPLE
IN THE NEWS

Princess Diana

by Walter Oleksy

Lucent Books, San Diego, CA

Library of Congress Cataloging-in-Publication Data

Oleksy, Walter G., 1930–
    Princess Diana / by Walter Oleksy.
        p.   cm. — (People in the News)
    Includes bibliographical references and index.
    Summary: The life of the Princess of Wales including her childhood, royal courtship and marriage, public and private life, divorce, humanitarian efforts, and untimely death.
    ISBN 1-56006-579-6 (lib. bdg. : alk. paper)
    1. Diana, Princess of Wales, 1961–1997—Juvenile literature. 2. Princesses—Great Britain—Biography—Juvenile literature. [1. Diana, Princess of Wales, 1961– 2. Princesses. 3. Women—Biography.]
I. Title. II. Series: People in the News (San Diego, Calif.)

DA591.A45 D53535   2000
941.085'092—dc21
                                                           99-053455

Copyright © 2000 by Lucent Books, Inc.
P.O. Box 289011
San Diego, CA 92198-9011
Printed in the U.S.A.

Table of Contents

Foreword

F AME AND CELEBRITY are alluring. People are drawn to those who walk in fame's spotlight, whether they are known for great accomplishments or for notorious deeds. The lives of the famous pique public interest and attract attention, perhaps because their experiences seem in some ways so different from, yet in other ways so similar to, our own.

Newspapers, magazines, and television regularly capitalize on this fascination with celebrity by running profiles of famous people. For example, television programs such as *Entertainment Tonight* devote all of their programming to stories about entertainment and entertainers. Magazines such as *People* fill their pages with stories of the private lives of famous people. Even newspapers, newsmagazines, and television news frequently delve into the lives of well-known personalities. Despite the number of articles and programs, few provide more than a superficial glimpse at their subjects.

Lucent's People in the News series offers young readers a deeper look into the lives of today's newsmakers, the influences that have shaped them, and the impact they have had in their fields of endeavor and on other people's lives. The subjects of the series hail from many disciplines and walks of life. They include authors, musicians, athletes, political leaders, entertainers, entrepreneurs, and others who have made a mark on modern life and who, in many cases, will continue to do so for years to come.

These biographies are more than factual chronicles. Each book emphasizes the contributions, accomplishments, or deeds that have brought fame or notoriety to the individual and shows how that person has influenced modern life. Authors portray their subjects in a realistic, unsentimental light. For example, Bill Gates—the cofounder and chief executive officer of the software giant Microsoft—has been instrumental in making personal computers the most vital tool of the modern age. Few dispute his business savvy, his perseverance, or his technical expertise, yet critics say he is ruthless in his dealings with competitors and driven more by his desire to maintain Microsoft's dominance in the computer industry than by an interest in furthering technology.

In these books, young readers will encounter inspiring stories about real people who achieved success despite enormous obstacles. Oprah Winfrey—the most powerful, most watched, and wealthiest woman on television today—spent the first six years of her life in the care of her grandparents while her unwed mother sought work and a better life elsewhere. Her adolescence was colored by promiscuity, pregnancy at age fourteen, rape, and sexual abuse.

Each author documents and supports his or her work with an array of primary and secondary source quotations taken from diaries, letters, speeches, and interviews. All quotes are footnoted to show readers exactly how and where biographers derive their information and provide guidance for further research. The quotations enliven the text by giving readers eyewitness views of the life and accomplishments of each person covered in the People in the News series.

In addition, each book in the series includes photographs, annotated bibliographies, timelines, and comprehensive indexes. For both the casual reader and the student researcher, the People in the News series offers insight into the lives of today's newsmakers—people who shape the way we live, work, and play in the modern age.

Princess and Humanitarian

Diana, Princess of Wales, was much loved by people all over the world. The compassion she showed the homeless, mentally ill, drug addicts, and the sick and disabled—both young and old—earned her a reputation as "the People's Princess." But despite an adoring public, Diana spent much of her life feeling alone, unwanted, and unloved.

As her prestige soared as the Princess of Wales, Diana grew correspondingly anguished in private. She complained that she could not bear to be the world megastar that she had become, yet at the same time she still scoured the newspapers for photographs of herself. It seemed to Diana's friends that she was searching for her own personal identity in the image of a princess smiling back at her from every front page.

Princess Diana was the most photographed and most written about woman in the world, but the media's excessive attention came at the cost of her privacy and peace of mind. She had anxieties about being a public figure and felt overwhelmed by her public responsibilities as wife of the future king of England. Insecurities borne of her parents' divorce when she was eight years old were compounded by the perception that her own marriage was loveless. She also felt at odds with the royal family's more distant approach to the public.

But as Diana struggled with depression, eating disorders, and a troubled marriage, she nonetheless reached out to others through her humanitarian work.

Princess Diana's compassion toward all people brought her the adoration of millions worldwide.

Her life, unfortunately, was like a fairy tale without a happy ending. Following the car accident that claimed her life at thirty-six years of age, the world mourned in a great outpouring of grief.

More than 1.5 million people lined the route of Diana's funeral procession through the streets of London to Westminster Abbey on Saturday morning, September 6, 1997. The funeral was the most watched event in television history. Over 2.5 billion people in more than sixty countries around the world—nearly half the population of Earth—watched the procession and funeral on live television.

Who Was Diana?

Andrew Morton, one of many writers who tried to understand who Diana was, wrote these thoughts about her in the concluding pages of the commemorative edition of his book *Diana: Her True Story:*

How then do we explain Diana the individual and Diana the phenomenon? In her life Diana was a complex web of contradictions; fearless yet frail, unloved but adored, needy but generous, self-obsessed yet selfless, inspirational yet despairing, demanding of advice but disliking criticism, intuitive yet unworldly, supremely sophisticated, yet constantly uncertain, and manipulative but naive.

She could be willful, exasperating, a flawed perfectionist who would disarm with a self-deprecating witticism; her penetrating cornflower-blue eyes seduced with a glance. Her language knew no boundaries; her lexicon [means of communication] was that of the smile, the caress, the hug and the kiss, not the statement of the speech. She was endlessly fascinating and will remain eternally enigmatic.[1]

Chapter 1

The Girlhood of a Princess

Diana Frances Spencer was born into a wealthy and aristocratic British family, but she suffered emotionally in her childhood when her parents divorced. When she was a teenager, she developed a schoolgirl crush on Charles, Prince of Wales.

Her less-than-idyllic childhood, which had caused her to feel unwanted and unloved, led her to search for a Prince Charming to love and care for her. She set up unrealistic expectations that perhaps marriage to Charles would bring her the happiness she felt she had so far been denied.

Born into a Conflicted Family

Diana was born on July 1, 1961, at the Spencer family's home, Park House. The large mansion had formerly been a hunting lodge on the royal family's eastern England estate near Sandringham, Norfolk. Diana's father rented Park House from Queen Elizabeth II, whom he served as an equerry, or aide.

Diana was the third daughter of John Spencer and Frances Ruth Burke Roche Spencer. John was a remote descendant of the Stuart kings of England, and Frances was the daughter of a wealthy Anglo-Irish baron. The Spencers were not a royal family, but they had become wealthy through sheep farming and had been in the service of the royal family for generations. For years Diana's grandmother Lady Ruth Fermoy was in personal service to the queen mother as chief lady-in-waiting.

Diana had two older sisters: Sarah, who was born in 1955, and Jane, who was born two years later. A brother, John, had

Diana's parents were John Spencer and Frances Ruth Burke Roche. The couple divorced in 1969 after many years of marital strife.

been born in 1960, but he was sickly and died only ten hours later. John Spencer became almost desperate that his next child be a son and heir. Instead, Diana, was born. This disappointment soon caused conflict in her parents' marriage and inflicted Diana with a sense of being unwanted and unloved.

Three years after Diana's birth, in 1964, Diana's mother gave birth to the long-awaited son and Spencer heir, whom they named Charles. But even his birth did not strengthen the Spencers' marriage.

Royal Neighbors

Diana and her siblings lived rather isolated in the old mansion in the country. As Mary Clarke, one of Diana's nannies, recalled, "The [Spencer] children were all brought up in a very old-fashioned way, as though they were still living at the turn of the century. . . . Very few friends came to the house; the children were expected to play together."[2]

Since the Spencers' home at Sandringham was next door to the royal family's summer residence, the children sometimes exchanged party invitations with their neighbors. Diana became a playmate of the queen's younger sons, Andrew and Edward, who joined swimming parties in the Spencers' pool, which was the only heated pool in the area.

Diana rarely saw the young royals' older brother, Prince Charles, because he was away at school. But family and friends began calling Diana "Duch," teasing that one day she would

Diana and Her Nannies

Diana and her brother Charles grew up in the care of nannies who lived in their parents' house at Sandringham and looked after the children's health, welfare, and preschooling. The two did not care for most of their nannies, as Diana later recalled in Andrew Morton's *Diana: Her True Story.*

> We had so many changes of nannies. My brother and I, if we didn't like them we used to stick pins in their chair and throw their clothes out the window. We always thought they were a threat because they tried to take mother's position. They were all rather young and pretty. They were chosen by my father. It was terribly disruptive to come back from school one day to find a new nanny.

Diana and her brother were capable of great mischief, and some of the nannies responded harshly. One nanny beat Diana on the head with a wooden spoon for being naughty; another banged Diana's and Charles's heads together. The children's misdeeds included taking Charles's pony upstairs into the nursery for grooming one day because they thought it was cold in the stables. When one nanny would not let Diana stay up past her bedtime, Diana locked the nanny in a bathroom. She did not let the woman out until her father came home to say goodnight to her and her brother.

marry Andrew, the duke of York, who was just a year older than she, and become a duchess. Diana didn't think so.

A Lonely Childhood

Diana's girlhood was lonely. Her sisters were away at school, her father was emotionally distant and did not show her affection, and her mother was unhappy because of her troubled marriage. As Diana recalled,

> My sisters—their growing up was done out of my sight. I saw them at holidays. I don't remember it being a big thing.

> I idolized my eldest sister [Sarah] and I used to do all her washing when she came back from school. I packed her suitcase, ran her bath, made her bed—the whole lot. I did it all and I thought it was wonderful. I always looked after my brother, really. My sisters were very independent.[3]

Diana's parents often argued. Their marital problems distressed Diana greatly, partly because she felt responsible by not having been born the son that her father had wanted so badly. A family friend, Peter Janson, later said that Diana's early years were horrible because of her parents' feuding. As he explained, "Her parents hated and despised each other by this time. [Diana] grew up in that kind of atmosphere."[4]

When she was six, Diana was sitting alone on the cold stone floor at Park House one night when she saw some of the domestic staff hurriedly loading her mother's things into a waiting car. Diana ran to a window and saw her mother enter the car and angrily slam the door shut. Diana claimed she never forgot the sound of the engine starting and the wheels scrunching over gravel as her mother drove off, the house falling deathly silent as she watched the car speed away. Her mother had left home, never to return.

Diana later explained how this affected her:

> The biggest disruption [to my childhood] was when Mummy decided to leg it [leave]. That's the vivid memory we have—the four of us [Diana, her two sisters, and her

brother]. We all have our own interpretations of what should have happened and what did happen. People took sides. Various people didn't speak to each other. For my brother and I it was a very wishy-washy and painful experience.[5]

A bitter two-year divorce and custody battle followed, which was reported on the front pages of newspapers throughout Great Britain. Much of the notoriety centered on Frances Spencer, who had left her husband and children to be with another man, the dashing wallpaper heir Peter Shand-Kydd.

Separation and Divorce

After fourteen years of marriage, the Spencers' divorce was finalized in 1969. Although Frances Spencer had fought for legal custody of her children, it was awarded to Diana's father. She was apparently denied custody because of her scandalous romance with another man.

Diana's mother remarried soon after the divorce and moved to Shand-Kydd's beef farm on an island in the remote northwest of Scotland, about 450 miles from London. Diana and her

Diana is seen here with Souffle, a Shetland pony, at her mother's home in Scotland.

brother continued to live with their father at Park House, but they visited their mother on school holidays.

Concerning her parents' divorce, Diana later said, "The divorce helped me to relate to anyone else who is upset in their family life, whether it be stepfather syndrome or mother or whatever, I understand it."[6] Diana became determined that when she would marry, what had happened to her parents' marriage would never happen to hers.

School Days

Until the age of nine, Diana was educated at home by the same governess who had tutored her mother. But in 1970, despite Diana's pleas, her father then sent her to Riddlesworth Hall Prep School near Diss, Norfolk. She often pleaded with him, "If you love me, you won't leave me here."[7]

But Diana remained at Riddlesworth until she was twelve. Then, following family tradition, she transferred to West Heath, a boarding school near Sevenoaks, Kent. Her mother and sisters had gone there before her, and Diana came to enjoy it. At West Heath she was regarded as a "thoroughly average" pupil, "a perfectly ordinary little girl who was always kind and cheerful."[8]

Diana played the piano at school and was active in sports, including swimming, tennis, volleyball, and hockey. Later, she recalled her school life:

> I always felt very different from everyone else, very detached. I knew I was going somewhere different but had no idea where. [I felt] generally unhappy and being very detached from everybody else. At the age of fourteen, I just remember thinking that I wasn't very good at anything, that I was hopeless.[9]

West Heath encouraged its students to become active in community service. Diana had an empathy for the lonely because of her own lonely childhood, so she chose to visit the elderly. "I visited old people once a week, went to the local mental asylum once a week," she later said. "I adored that."[10]

Diana also developed a talent for swimming, a passion for ballet, and an infatuation with Prince Charles. She hung his pho-

In Trouble at School

Diana was not always a well-behaved pupil at Riddlesworth Hall, the preparatory school in Norfolk where she lived and studied from ages eleven to thirteen. She revealed her troubles in school in "In Her Own Words," published as the foreword to the commemorative edition of her biography by Andrew Morton, *Diana: Her True Story*.

I nearly got expelled because one night somebody said to me: "'Would I like to do a dare?" I thought "Why not? Life's so boring." So they sent me out at 9 o'clock to the end of the drive which was half a mile long in pitch dark. I had to go and get some sweets at the gate from somebody called Polly Phillimore. I got there and there was nobody there.

I hid behind the gate as these police cars were coming in. I thought nothing more about it. I saw all the lights coming on in the school. I thought some twit in my bedroom said that she had appendicitis. Then they asked "Where's Diana?" "Don't know." Both parents, then divorced, were summoned. Father was thrilled and my mother said: "I didn't think you had it in you." No telling off. . . . I wasn't a good child in the sense that I had horns in my ears. I was always looking for trouble.

As a young schoolgirl, Diana was often getting into trouble.

tograph above her cot and told classmates, "I would love to be a dancer—or Princess of Wales."[11]

Diana Becomes a Lady

In 1975 Diana's grandfather John "Jack" Spencer, the seventh Earl Spencer, died at the age of eighty-three. Her father inherited his title and estate, becoming the eighth Earl Spencer. At the age of fourteen, Diana became Lady Diana Spencer. The family moved into the ancestral Spencer mansion on an estate at Althorp (pronounced "Al-trup"), located about seventy-five miles northwest of London.

Before long her father remarried, and Diana had a stepmother. Raine Legge, a divorcée, was the former countess of Dartmouth and the daughter of romance novelist Barbara Cartland. Diana and her siblings resented their stepmother. They feared that Legge was trying to take their mother's place, and they were jealous of the attention their father gave to his new wife. As Mary Clarke recalled, "The children didn't want to share him with a new mother."[12]

Diana's father inherited the Spencer mansion at Althorp (pictured) after her grandfather's death in 1975.

Diana Meets the Prince of Wales

Diana's schoolgirl infatuation with Prince Charles soon took her mind off of her stepmother. While at school in November 1977, when Diana was sixteen, she was given a special weekend pass to go home to Althorp to attend a pheasant-shooting party. The guest of honor was Prince Charles, who was then dating Diana's eldest sister, Sarah.

In search of a potential wife, the twenty-eight-year-old Charles had been dating a lot of beautiful women. But most people could see that his relationship with Sarah Spencer, who was considered the dynamic rebel of the three Spencer girls, was not going anywhere. They simply were not falling in love with each other.

As Sarah explained: "He's [Prince Charles] a fabulous person, but I'm not in love with him. I think of him as the big brother I never had."[13]

Sarah introduced Diana to the prince in the middle of a field on the Althorp estate during a bleak afternoon of pheasant shooting. Diana thought she did not cut a very impressive figure in a checkered shirt, corduroy pants, and boots. She later recalled their meeting:

> I remember being a fat, podgy, no makeup unsmart lady, but I made a lot of noise and he liked that and he came up to me after dinner and we had a big dance. . . . He was charm himself. . . . For someone like that to show you any attention—I was just so sort of amazed.[14]

Charles later described his impression of Diana that weekend: "What a jolly and amusing and attractive sixteen-year-old. I mean great fun—bouncy and full of life and everything."[15] That impression came to Charles, in part, because Diana showed him how to tap dance that weekend.

Although impressed, Charles thought Diana was too young to consider as a marriage prospect. For Diana, her meeting with Prince Charles that weekend was much more. According to Penny Walker, Diana's piano teacher at West Heath,

> Diana adored Prince Charles for years and years. She had photos of him everywhere in her bedroom and her dream was to come face to face with him.

I remember her coming back to school after a weekend home and telling me, "I've met him. I've met him at last!" Her dream had come true.[16]

A Yearning for Independence

At about this time, Diana, who was not scholarly, wanted to drop out of school and live with her mother. She hoped it could be the start of a more independent life for herself.

Her mother's second marriage had ended by this time, and she had taken an apartment in London. Diana's father agreed that she could leave West Heath, but he opposed her living with her mother. Instead, he sent her to the Institut Alpin Videmanette, an expensive "finishing" school in Rougemont, Switzerland, where girls prepared for becoming young ladies in classes that taught, among other things, etiquette and social graces.

But Diana was unhappy there and pleaded with her father to let her return to London and live with her mother. Again, because he disapproved of his former wife's lifestyle, he only partly relented. Diana could return to London, but not to live with her mother.

With some money she inherited, Diana bought a three bedroom apartment in London. She shared housekeeping and cooking duties with three female roommates. Determined to find a job and begin an independent life of her own, Diana became a caretaker for an elderly woman, a nanny for an American girl, and then a kindergarten teacher's aide.

Kay King, who also worked at the kindergarten, later discussed Diana's work there: "Di was shy with adults but had this incredible ability with children to get down to their level. She always looked for the children that were unhappy. She was such fun, which children respond to."[17]

Independence agreed with Diana. She enjoyed the freedom of having a job she liked and an apartment in London. She had also outgrown her "podginess" by then and was becoming a tall, slender beauty. As her brother, Charles, later recalled, "Suddenly the insignificant ugly duckling was obviously going to be a swan."[18]

Chapter 2

A Royal Courtship and Marriage

Dᴵᴬᴺᴬ ᴡᴬˢ ᴄᴇʀᴛᴀɪɴ that she had found her Prince Charming in Charles, Prince of Wales. Charles, likewise, believed that the beautiful and vivacious young aristocrat fulfilled his requirements in a wife. After a courtship covered extensively in the media, their wedding of pomp and ceremony was unequaled in anyone's memory. The archbishop of Canterbury, who presided over the ceremony, called the marriage the "stuff of which fairy tales are made." [19]

A Royal Romance

The spark of romance between Charles and Diana began in July 1980, when both attended a small house party in Petworth that was hosted by their mutual friends Commander Robert de Pass and his wife, Philippa, who was a lady-in-waiting to the queen.

Diana had driven to Petworth and watched Charles play polo. Afterward, she attended the barbecue at the de Pass estate, where she was seated on a hay bale beside the prince. He was still despondent over the assassination of his adored uncle, Lord Earl Mountbatten, the year before. Mountbatten had been Charles's confidant, and the prince missed him greatly. Diana had been invited to the party because her friends thought Charles needed cheering up.

Rather than try to amuse Charles, however, Diana consoled him. Charles was deeply moved by Diana's compassion, and when he had to return to Buckingham Palace to attend to important paperwork the next morning, he asked her to drive back to London with him. Diana politely refused saying it would be rude to her hosts to leave earlier than they expected.

The relationship had begun. One of her roommates recalled later, "Prince Charles was coming quietly on to the scene. [Diana] certainly had a special place for him in her heart."[20]

On Diana's first date with Charles, they went to the Royal Albert Hall for a Sunday evening performance of *Requiem,* a solemn symphony for the dead that was one of Charles's favorite classical works. Diana's grandmother Lady Ruth Fermoy accompanied them as chaperone to the concert and to a cold buffet supper afterward in Charles's apartment at Buckingham Palace.

Charles then invited Diana to join him on the royal yacht, *Britannia,* during the annual August regatta, or sailing races. Perhaps to distance herself from gossip on the weekend, she went waterskiing while Charles went windsurfing.

Ever since she was a young girl, Diana hoped to meet and eventually marry Charles, Prince of Wales.

Within a month, Charles asked Diana to join him at Balmoral, his mother's highland castle in Scotland, for the Braemar Games (Scottish sporting events) in September. Diana accepted, and Charles was attentive to her over the weekend, inviting her to join him for a walk and a barbecue.

Diana enjoyed the weekend until a newspaper reporter-photographer, named James Whitaker, who had been keeping watch for a possible budding romance between the prince and any new young woman, spotted them through binoculars while Charles was fishing. Diana, thoughtful of the prince's privacy, hid behind a tree while Charles continued fishing.

Cleverly, Diana used the mirror in her powder compact to watch the journalist. She waited in hiding for half an hour, hoping that Whitaker and the other photographers who had joined him would give up and go away. When they did not, she disguised herself in a scarf and flat cap so that they could not guess her identity. She fooled them by strolling casually away into a forest of pine trees.

Recalling his time with Diana at Balmoral, Charles said, "I began to realize what was going on in my mind and hers in particular." [21]

Some observers said that Diana had set her cap for Charles at Balmoral. One of them who observed her that weekend said, "Diana set out to be noticed. She's very good at attracting attention, and she made sure she attracted the Prince of Wales." [22]

In the Spotlight

When reporters and photographers discovered who the new mystery girl was in Prince Charles's life, they all but camped out in front of Diana's London apartment to ask her questions and photograph her. She held them off at first, but after badgering her at the kindergarten where she worked, she agreed to let them photograph her if they would then let her alone. They agreed and she was photographed with some of the children outside the kindergarten.

Diana thought the photo session was innocent enough until she saw herself on the front pages of tabloid newspapers and was

Prince Charles

Charles and Diana may not have had shared many interests, but both had unhappy childhoods that strongly influenced their adult lives.

Prince Charles, whose full name was Charles Philip Arthur George, was born on November 14, 1948, at Buckingham Palace in London, the first child of Queen Elizabeth II and Philip Mountbatten, the duke of Edinburgh.

Like Diana, Charles was brought up not by his mother but by royal nannies or nursery maids. When he was an infant, his mother saw him only twice a day: when he was carried to her after breakfast for thirty minutes, then for another half hour just before his bedtime. Weeks would pass without him seeing his father, who was then an officer in the Royal Navy and was away at sea. When his father was home, Charles found him to be either stern or remote. His father also believed that children, even at an early age, should be independent and fend for themselves.

Biographers have said that Charles never really enjoyed his home life as a child or as a teenager. He was away at school a lot, and when he was home, he and his parents were distant, although he was in awe of his mother, the queen.

Like Diana, Charles frequently heard his parents argue. Later, the couple took up separate suites at opposite ends of Buckingham Palace. They did not, however, divorce.

Also like Diana, Charles was sent away to school at an early age. He was tutored at Buckingham Palace until he was nine, then he was sent to a boarding school near London. He later studied in Australia and then spent three years at Cambridge studying history, archaeology, and anthropology. After graduation, he trained as a pilot in the Royal Air Force, but he later joined the Royal Navy.

In later years, Charles became interested in architecture, painting, organic gardening, and Oriental religion. In 1976 he organized the Prince's Trust, which helped unemployed and poor Britons start their own small businesses. Prince Charles was praised for his charitable works and for helping and shaking hands with the underprivileged, as his future wife, Diana, would also be.

shocked. She had worn a cotton skirt and photographers had snapped their camera shutters when the light was behind her, so her dress looked transparent, revealing her legs.

Though the photos distressed Diana, Charles made light of them, saying, "I knew your legs were good, but I didn't realize they were that spectacular." He then kidded, "And did you really have to show them to everybody?" [23]

Almost overnight, Charles and Diana's courtship became an international obsession with the public and the media. The media clamored to learn if Charles and Diana would marry.

Over the next few months, Prince Charles divided his time between seeing Diana and going out of the country on royal engagements, such as to India and Nepal. Although he was often away, he was certain to telephone her.

The Proposal

On February 4, 1981, Charles asked Diana to have dinner with him in his apartment at Buckingham Palace. They dined alone in his book-cluttered blue sitting room. Later that night in the castle nursery where he had played as a child, Charles asked Diana to marry him.

Diana was nervous. Her first reaction was to take the proposal lightheartedly. She giggled. Then she saw that he was serious and accepted his proposal, repeatedly telling him she loved him. He reportedly replied, "Whatever love means."[24]

Once her relationship with Charles became public knowledge, Diana found it increasingly difficult to avoid the press.

"It wasn't a difficult decision," Diana said later. "It was what I wanted."[25]

After Diana accepted Charles's proposal of marriage that night, she returned to her apartment, flopped down on her bed, and teased her friends.

"Guess what?" she asked. Her friends cried out, "He asked you!" Diana replied, "He did, and I said, 'Yes please.'" One of her friends remembered, "We started to squeal with excitement. Then we burst into floods of tears."[26]

Diana told her friends that now, for the first time in her life, she felt secure. She was certain that she was going to marry without the fear that her husband would leave her, and her marriage would not, like her parents', end in divorce.

Despite Diana's acceptance of his marriage proposal, Charles thought she might need more time to consider the responsibilities she would take on as his wife and the likely future queen of England. He suggested that she think his proposal over

Prince Charles on Marriage

At one time considered the most eligible bachelor in the world, the Prince of Wales publicly acknowledged that he thought thirty was a good age to settle down. This excerpt, which is taken from Andrew Morton's *Diana: Her True Story*, relates the royal bachelor's opinion of marriage when he was thirty-two.

> Marriage is a much more important business than falling in love. I think one must concentrate on marriage being essentially a question of mutual love and respect for each other. . . . Essentially you must be good friends, and love, I'm sure, will grow out of that friendship. I have a particular responsibility to ensure that I make the right decision. The last thing I could possibly entertain is getting divorced.

In her book *Diana, Princess of Wales*, Penny Junor also discusses Charles's pragmatic view of marriage.

> A woman not only marries a man; she marries into a way of life —a job. She's got to have some knowledge of it, some sense of it; otherwise she wouldn't have a clue about whether she's going to like it. If I'm deciding on whom I want to live with for fifty years—well, that's the last decision on which I want my head to be ruled by my heart. . . . To me, marriage seems to be the biggest and most responsible step to be taken in one's life.

and give her answer again upon returning from a trip to Australia that she had previously planned with her mother.

Diana received neither a telephone call nor a wire from Charles while she was away nearly two weeks. Upon her return to London, there was no note from him. Still, Diana was in love, and though only nineteen years old, she was confident that with his help she could handle the duties of the Princess of Wales. When she saw him again, she accepted his proposal a second time. As she told reporters after her engagement, "With Prince Charles beside me, I can't go wrong."[27]

The Engagement

After receiving the enthusiastic approval of their families, the engagement of Charles, the Prince of Wales, and Lady Diana Spencer was made public on February 24, 1981. Lord Chamberlain made the announcement to a roomful of royal friends and dignitaries at Buckingham Palace, and in no time the engagement made news all over the world.

At almost the same moment as the announcement of the royal engagement was made, three policemen took up guard in front of Diana's apartment building. She was already regarded as being royal.

Many people who knew both Diana and Charles were surprised when they became engaged because they did not share the same interests. He, for example, liked to read philosophical books while she favored a good story. He loved horseback riding and polo; she preferred swimming. He liked opera and classical music, but she liked ballet and rock and roll. Charles loved the country and simple outdoor pleasures such as gardening while Diana preferred the city life with its parties and dances.

When television reporters asked the couple how they felt about their engagement in their first interview together, Diana appeared to be deliriously happy while Charles remained his restrained self.

One reporter asked whether they were in love. "Of course!" Diana said, smiling shyly. "Whatever 'in love' means,"[28] Charles said with a doubtful expression, repeating the words he had said after proposing to her. Diana was visibly disappointed by his remark.

Diana and Prince Charles announce their engagement after Queen Elizabeth II gave her formal consent for the couple to marry.

Diana could not have known it at the time of her engagement, but while she was in love with Charles, he apparently was unsure about his feelings for her. As he had confided to a friend, "I expect it will be the right thing in the end. I do very much want to do the right thing for this country and for my family. But I'm terrified sometimes of making a promise and then perhaps living to regret it."[29]

Photographers and reporters immediately began to follow Diana wherever she went. She resigned her kindergarten job and was offered sanctuary from the press in Clarence House, the queen mother's (Charles's grandmother's) residence in Buckingham Palace. It was rumored later that she was sent there so the queen mother could instruct her in the duties and protocol of being the Princess of Wales. Biographer Andrew Morton later debunked that theory, writing, "In reality, Diana was given less training in her new job than the average supermarket checkout operator."[30]

Diana had hoped that her future husband would be in London during their engagement, but more often he was away on royal business. On one such five-week state visit to Australia, Diana broke down and wept as she watched his airplane taxi away. The moment, caught on film and put on newspaper front pages, further endeared her to the public.

So, too, did the people love Diana's public display of compassion. Six days before her wedding, she visited some disabled elderly in London and showed them her engagement ring. When she realized that one of the women was blind, Diana asked her, "Do you want to feel my engagement ring? I'd better not lose it before Wednesday, or they won't know who I am."[31]

The Wedding

On the eve of Diana's wedding day, Charles sent his bride an affectionate note that read, "I'm so proud of you, and when you come up [the aisle] I'll be there at the altar for you tomorrow. Just look 'em in the eye and knock 'em dead."[32]

For her wedding the next morning, Diana did just that. After the hairdresser and makeup artist were finished with her, Diana looked radiant in her ivory silk taffeta wedding gown, veil, and twenty-five-foot-long train. Her brother, Charles, later recalled,

She was never one for makeup but she did look fantastic. It was the first time in my life I ever thought of Diana as beautiful. She really did look stunning that day and very composed, not showing any nerves although she was slightly pale. She was happy and calm.[33]

Like Cinderella, Diana rode in a horse-drawn glass coach from Clarence House to her wedding at St. Paul's Cathedral. Carrying a bouquet of gardenias, lilies of the valley, white freesia, golden roses, white orchids, and stephanotis, she entered the cathedral attended by five bridesmaids.

The earl of Spencer gave his daughter away at the ceremony. Recovering from a near-fatal stroke he had suffered several weeks before, he leaned heavily on Diana's arm as they began walking slowly side-by-side down the aisle. Diana faltered a step, but her unsteady father steadied her.

The archbishop of Canterbury, along with 25 other clerics, officiated at the wedding on July 29, 1981. Some 2,500 guests

Millions of people watched the fairy tale-like wedding of Diana and Prince Charles on July 29, 1981.

watched the ceremony inside St. Paul's Cathedral, over 600,000 spectators gathered outside, and about 100 million people from more than seventy countries around the world either watched the event on live television or listened to it on the radio.

Diana thought she got everything right during the ceremony, but she was unaware that she had repeated the groom's first and middle names out of sequence. When the minister asked if she would take "Charles Philip Arthur George for her wedded husband," she replied, "I, Diana, take thee Philip Charles Arthur George to be my wedded husband." [34]

Prince Andrew, who was standing nearby, thought it was a great joke when the bride muddled up the names of his older brother. "She's just married my father," [35] he quipped in a whisper.

After the ceremony, the newlyweds rode to Buckingham Palace in an elaborate open carriage drawn by four white horses while throngs of well-wishers on the streets cheered them. Soon they were on the palace balcony, and Diana knew what the crowd was urging. "They want us to kiss," she told her husband. "Why not?"[36] he replied. So she kissed him.

As the newlyweds departed for a honeymoon aboard the royal yacht, which included a twelve-day cruise through the Mediterranean to Egypt before returning to Balmoral in Scotland, people around the world went to sleep having witnessed the largest and most elaborate wedding ceremony ever mounted in the history of the British monarchy. Many called it the wedding of the century.

Chapter 3

The Public Princess

Dᴵᴬᴺᴬ ʙʟᴏssᴏᴹᴇᴅ ꜰʀᴏᴹ an insecure and shy high-school dropout into a beautiful, high-fashion, assured-looking adult, becoming the most popular woman in the world. Outwardly, she appeared to be a happy woman, successfully carrying out her personal responsibilities as a loving wife and mother while also fulfilling her public duties as the Princess of Wales. She was soon to learn that a great deal of pressure and stress came with performing those multiple tasks.

The Young Marrieds

Upon returning from their honeymoon on August 15, 1981, Charles and Diana took up residence in an apartment in Kensington Palace in London. It consisted of two guest rooms, a nursery, and servants' rooms besides a master bedroom suite, dining room, and three reception rooms. Other royals, including Princess Margaret, also had rooms in the palace.

Diana immediately immersed herself in her public duties as Princess of Wales, joining her husband at official functions as a representative of the queen. During her first year as princess, she was scheduled for 170 official engagements. These included everything from attending royal dinners at Buckingham Palace with visiting foreign dignitaries to cutting ribbons at ceremonial tree plantings.

As Princess of Wales, Diana was aware that her public image was very important. For one thing, tradition dictated that she was obliged to walk behind her husband—never ahead of or even beside him. It was also expected that she wear a hat when with the prince in public.

To help her learn the protocol of her new position and fine-tune her appearance, Diana looked to other members of the royal family as well as to hired fashion and makeup consultants. In no time, Diana became a darling of the fashion industry, wearing British-made clothes to public functions. Her shorter, sportier hairstyle became known as "the Princess Diana haircut" and was copied by many women around the world. Diana's new look and lively, more confident public persona were a hit.

On October 27 of that year, the royal couple began a three-day tour of Wales. Even in the rain, crowds cheered the new Princess of Wales.

The Pressures of a Prince and Princess

Diana had assured Charles when they became engaged that she could handle the duties of being the wife of the Prince of Wales. However, she had not really been aware of how great the pressures

After her wedding, Diana immediately immersed herself in her public duties as Princess of Wales.

and stress of her duties as Princess of Wales or her marriage to the future king of England would be, or how they would affect her.

One of Prince Charles's private secretaries later explained how stressful the tasks that Diana had agreed to undertake really were:

> I've never succeeded in describing to anybody who wasn't in the middle of it, the pressures of that life and that relationship. Almost any human being would have found it absolutely intolerable. Wherever you happened to be, every look, every gaze, every smile, every scowl, every hand you held or touched, under the microscope every time, front page news in the tabloids day after day . . . everybody after you. It was the most extraordinary pressure. . . .
>
> There wasn't much respite and that clearly took its toll on [Diana]. It takes its toll on [Prince Charles] too, but he's been brought up to it and developed his own defense mechanisms.[37]

As Prince of Wales and the heir to the throne, Charles had pressures of his own. Besides those of his public duties, Diana, who was jealous of his attachments to others, insisted that he give up many of his friends and aides. To placate her, he gave

Diana Learns Her Job

In the first years of her marriage, Diana's life was not all parties and hospital visits. She had a lot to learn in her new job as Princess of Wales, and she did her best to learn it all.

Diana learned many things from Princess Margaret and by watching other royal women in the palace. One trick she picked up from them was to sew tiny weights in the hem of her skirts, so the wind wouldn't blow them up. This was especially helpful when she was photographed on windy days.

Diana also needed to know how to handle herself and take care of her children in a dangerous situation. She learned this by taking anti-terrorism training from the British Special Air Services, Britain's equivalent of the U.S. Navy SEALs and the U.S. Army Special Forces combined. In one lesson, Diana drove her car through a course with flash grenades and smoke bombs exploding all around her. She even learned to use a .38mm pistol and a machine gun.

up many of his friends, his valet, and aides. He even gave up his dog, Harvey, a big yellow Labrador that he had traveled everywhere with and took along on hunting trips. Early in their marriage, Diana told Charles that the dog was associated with his past and with his friends, and she couldn't have it around. Reluctantly, Charles sent his dog off to live with an aide.

Diana and the Media

Even before her engagement to Prince Charles, Diana had found it distressing that reporters and photographers intruded on her private life. Early on, the media dubbed her "Shy Di." She did not like being called shy, and hated being called Di.

"Please don't call me that," she asked reporters and the public. "I've never been called Di. I really don't like it."[38] Yet, her wishes were ignored as she became more simply and familiarly known as Di.

In addition to disrespecting her feelings, some in the media criticized Diana for spending too much money—namely, on clothes. It has been pointed out that between 1981 and 1994, she had spent more than $2 million on her wardrobe, which included more than three thousand outfits, several hundred ball gowns, six hundred pairs of shoes, and four hundred hats.

Diana defended herself by saying that she had to look good if she was to represent the queen and her country at public functions:

> On the day we got engaged I literally had one long dress, one silk shirt, one smart pair of shoes, and that was it. Suddenly my mother and I had to go and buy six of everything. . . . Bear in mind [as Princess of Wales] you have to change four times a day and suddenly your wardrobe expands to something unbelievable.[39]

Although Diana enjoyed the attention she received as a leader of high fashion, it came at the sacrifice of something more important that she wanted from people. As she once explained, "I always used to think people just looked at my clothes and I was desperate for the other side to come out and be dealt with and didn't know how to do it."[40]

Most of Diana's troubles with members of the media, however, were caused by their constant attention. Dozens or more reporters and photographers followed Diana everywhere she went. Front pages of newspapers ran photos of her hugging sick children or merely shopping or getting into or out of a car. She could hardly believe the attention she was getting from the public and the media.

Even before her engagement, Diana had tried to find ways to escape the media. Back then, in fact, the only way that she could leave her apartment without reporters and photographers seeing her was to take the sheets off her bed and climb out a kitchen window. Most often, she was helpless to do anything about the harassment:

> I was constantly polite, constantly civil [to the media]. I was never rude. I never shouted [for them to leave me

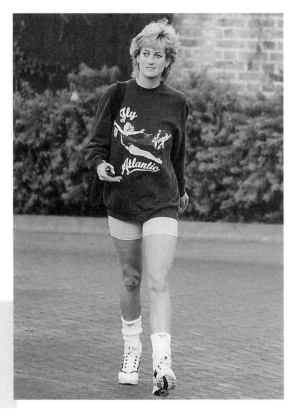

With the media following her every move, Diana found it impossible to relax or spend time by herself.

alone]. I cried like a baby to the four walls [when I was alone]. I just couldn't cope with it. I cried because I got no support from Charles and no support from the Palace press office. They just said, "You're on your own."[41]

Media hunger for news and photos of Diana intensified after her marriage. Photographers could earn thousands of dollars by selling pictures of her to newspapers and magazines. Because of this, Diana began to feel more like a product than a person. Sometimes the media harassment forced her to cancel social engagements because she felt "too distraught to leave my home."[42]

Critics have said that they do not think Diana fully understood the lack of privacy she would face by becoming Charles's wife and England's Princess Di. In a sense, said James Whitaker, the London *Mirror*'s royal reporter, "She didn't know she was marrying us, too."[43]

Motherhood

As Diana began to perform her public duties soon after her marriage to Charles, she was keenly aware that her most important duty as wife of the future king was to produce a son and heir. On November 5, 1981, it was announced from Buckingham Palace that the princess was expecting a child. Public interest and media attention on Diana, which were already high, reached a frenzy.

On June 21, 1982, Diana gave birth to a son who, after his father, was second in line to inherit the British throne. Prince Charles remained with his wife during the thirteen-hour period of labor and birth.

While Charles wanted his son to be named Arthur, Diana won the name game and their first child was christened William Arthur Philip Louis, officially to be known as Prince William of Wales. His parents would just call him "Will."

Two years later, the second son, Prince Henry Charles Albert David, was born to the royal couple on September 15, 1984. "Harry," together with his older brother, became known as "the Heir and the Spare."

Diana was a loving, doting mother. While Charles wanted their sons to be left in the care of nannies, Diana wanted to

spend as much time with her children as possible while still fulfilling her obligations as Princess of Wales.

Diana wanted her sons raised as normally as possible, telling
them, as her father had told her, that even though they were of
privileged birth, they were no better than anyone else. To that
end, she would try to raise her boys away from prying reporters
and cameramen, but she found that difficult if not impossible.

After Harry's birth, as Diana's popularity skyrocketed between 1984 and 1986, the public cheered her and the media followed her even more. Charles was admittedly jealous of the
attention paid to his wife, telling a friend, "It's only Diana they
want now. I don't count anymore."[44]

Charles noticed something else that distressed him about the
media's love affair with his wife. Although reporters were
mainly positive in writing about her, he believed it was not the

*Diana was determined to
spend as much time as
possible with her sons
Prince William (seated)
and Prince Harry.*

same when they wrote about him. As Penny Junor later wrote in *Charles: Victim or Villain?*,

> [Prince Charles] had grown bitterly disillusioned about the media during the course of his marriage. He felt, not without some justification, that it had short-changed him. In the early days [of his marriage] he had been ignored in favor of his wife. [Later, the media] chipped away remorselessly. They printed story after story which condemned or ridiculed him.[45]

Charles may or may not have realized that the public cheered Diana more and the media wrote more favorably of her because she demonstrated more natural warmth and affection than he did.

Realizing that she was getting more media attention than her husband, at times Diana tried to move the cameras onto Charles by wearing the same dress many times during a year. A photographer once griped, "Damn! The old pink [dress] again. She's wearing her old clothes to try to shift the spotlight onto *him,* and it won't work!"[46]

Diana the Humanitarian

In the first eight years of her marriage, Diana divided her time between being a wife and mother and attending charity balls, official dinners, and public ceremonies. In 1989 a new phase of her life began that was more personally important to her as she expanded her public appearances to include visiting hospitals to cheer up sick or disabled children and the elderly.

"I was very confused by which area I should go into," Diana said about wondering what volunteer work to do. "Then I found myself being more and more involved with people who were rejected by society . . . and I found an affinity there."[47]

This concern gradually led Diana to visit alcohol and drug abusers and the homeless. Soon she was showing compassion for AIDS victims by hugging them or holding their hands. At a time when AIDS patients were stigmatized and people were afraid to touch them, some people thought that Diana risked her

Diana Learns the Healing of Touch

When Diana visited the elderly, the sick, and disabled children while doing community service work as a teenager at West Heath, she learned
how a touch can comfort those in need. Diana learned this from Muriel
Stevens, who worked with the school's hospital voluntary services.
Stevens later recalled her time with Diana in "Diana, Her True Story,"
an episode of Arts and Entertainment's program *Biography*.

> The first thing I taught Diana was to stoop down so she was al-
> ways on [the patient's] eye level. It was important because
> many were in wheelchairs. The second thing was to always get
> hold of their hands. An instant physical contact. It also meant
> that for a young person like Di who was very pretty, patients
> would want to touch her face.

As the Princess of Wales, Diana would spend countless hours in the
hospitals visiting the elderly, sick, and disabled.

life doing this, but she did not allow public misconception to de-
ter her.

"I had always wanted to hug people in hospital beds," Diana
recalled.

> This particular man [a young AIDS patient] who was so
> ill started crying when I sat on his bed. He held my hand
> and I thought, "Diana, do it, just do it," and I gave him
> an enormous hug. It was just so touching because he
> clung to me and he cried.[48]

An Effort for Understanding

Diana sometimes took her sons with her visiting the sick and disadvantaged. "I take them around homeless projects," she said. "I've taken William and Harry to people dying of AIDS, although I told them it was cancer. I want them to have an understanding of people's emotions, people's insecurities, of people's hopes and dreams."[49]

Diana increased her work with AIDS patients in 1991 by visiting more AIDS shelters. "She would look you in the eye when she arrived as if to say, 'I'm yours for the evening. What do you want me to do?'" said Michael Watson, former chairman of the AIDS Charity Crusaid in London. "If she had to stand on her head for you, she would do it."[50]

Diana's presence among AIDS victims was worth even more than her fund-raising efforts for them. Margaret Jay, director of Britain's National AIDS Trust, said Diana's great contribution was in "influencing attitudes. Her speech saying AIDS involved everyone . . . was worth hundreds of millions in ads."[51]

By showing her compassion for AIDS victims, Diana demonstrated that it was safe to show care for them.

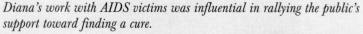

Diana's work with AIDS victims was influential in rallying the public's support toward finding a cure.

A Change Comes Over the Princess

Diana noticeably gained confidence from her volunteer work. As one of her closest advisers said, "Diana is on a voyage of discovery at the moment. What we are seeing is her real personality coming through. . . . She will make mistakes, but ultimately we will see a genuine manifestation of the real person."[52]

Another person who noticed Diana's growing confidence was a nurse named Oonagh Toffolo, who sometimes cared for Diana. Toffolo recalled that Diana had previously been timid and would not look her straight in the eye. "Over the last two years [since Diana began doing humanitarian work]," Toffolo said, "she has got in touch with her own nature and has found a new confidence and sense of liberation which she had never known before."[53]

One of Diana's best friends, Angela Serota, a dancer with the Royal Ballet, also noticed a change in Diana after the princess began doing volunteer work. "I thought she was utterly beautiful in a very profound way. She has an inner spirit which shines forth though there was also a sense of pervasive unhappiness about her."[54]

But while Diana showed an increase in self-confidence, by 1990 she also showed strains of nine years in a marriage in which she felt unloved and in a world spotlight she could no longer tolerate. She could no longer hide her growing annoyance with the media or her anxieties concerning her marriage. Reporters and the public began to notice a coolness between the royal couple when they were together at events.

When the couple visited India together in February 1992, Diana chose to pose alone in front of the Taj Mahal. A photo of her sitting without her husband in front of one of the world's major symbols of love began to make the public suspect that the marriage was in trouble.

Charles's biographer, Jonathan Dimbleby, writes about this in *The Prince of Wales:*

> The photo opportunity at the Taj Mahal provided an ironic if unintended symbol: poised before one of the world's greatest monuments to love, the image both sug-

gested an unbearable isolation and administered a fearsome rebuke to a loveless and errant husband."[55]

In the same book, Dimbleby says that Charles told him that he usually tried to console Diana when she was upset. Dimbleby said Charles felt tenderness and pity when Diana was stricken by what he called her moods.

At about this time, Charles also revealed to a friend that he despaired that his wife could not be "a friend" to him, and he considered canceling future public appearances: "The strain is immense, and yet I want to do my duty in the way I've been trained. I feel so unsuited to the ghastly business of human intrigue and general nastiness. . . . I don't know what will happen from now on, but I dread it."[56]

Diana's choice to pose alone in front of the Taj Mahal fueled rumors of marital trouble.

Rumors of marital problems were rampant in the following months, and the glum expressions on their faces and their open coolness to each other on a visit to South Korea that November confirmed the public's suspicions. The royal couple was no longer in love—at least, not with each other.

If Diana had not yet found herself in her humanitarian work, she was on her way there. Yet, as her friend Angela Serota observed, there was another side of Diana that the princess kept locked in her heart. Her public image was one thing, but her private self was another.

Chapter 4

The Private Princess

PUBLICLY, DIANA APPEARED to be a cheerful, energetic, positive princess. Privately, however, she suffered many anxieties and heartaches that at times overwhelmed her and drove her to emotional and physical illness. Her private anxieties could be classified as marriage, royalty, eating, and friendship troubles. No one but Diana knew the price she was paying to be the Princess of Wales. At the root of her problems was a lifelong sense of insecurity and inferiority that made her believe she was not good enough.

The Two Sides of Diana

Dealing with the pressures and stresses of her life as the Princess of Wales during ten years of marriage, Diana was well aware of and much distressed by the two conflicting sides of her life. As she wrote in her notes for *Diana: Her True Story,*

> The public side was very different from the private side. The public side, they [people] wanted a fairy princess to come and touch them and everything will turn into gold and all their worries would be forgotten. Little did they realize that the individual was crucifying herself inside, because she didn't think she was good enough.[57]

Royal Troubles

Diana had been born into Britain's aristocracy, but not its royalty. After she married Prince Charles and became a princess, she grew anxious about the royal life she then had to live. "I hadn't got enough background on what the Princess of Wales was supposed to do,"[58] she later said.

As she wrote in notes to her biographer, Andrew Morton,

> When I first arrived on the [royal] scene . . . I was just so frightened of the attention I was getting. . . . It was too much for one person at that time. . . .

> I didn't want to do anything on my own. I was too frightened. The thought of me doing anything on my own sent tremors, so I stuck with whatever Charles did.[59]

Diana found it difficult to adjust to the royals' routine at Buckingham Palace, Windsor Castle, and at Balmoral, the queen's residence in Scotland. For one thing, Diana had been used to eating quick dinners and then rushing off to whatever she wanted. Even before her marriage to Charles, their dinners with the queen and others in the royal family often took several hours, depending on the guests and conversation. Diana became bored and impatient at them, then distressed when she realized that the long, formal rituals would take place every night that they dined with the queen, which was often.

After one of the dinners at Balmoral, Diana wrote to a friend, "I feel totally out of place here. I sometimes wonder what on earth I've gotten myself into. I feel so small, so lonely, so out of my depth. . . . All I can talk about with them is the bloody weather!"[60]

Another time, Diana complained to one of Charles's friends, "No one talks to me. I stand around at every official gathering not knowing what to do, what to say, or where to look. I'm worried that I might do something wrong, and I feel like a fish out of water."[61]

Sometimes Diana would visit the domestic help downstairs, where she found it easier to relax. One day at Balmoral when she went downstairs to hang around the kitchen and talk to the servants, they were embarrassed.

A senior house staff member took her aside once and said, "I must ask you not to come down here again, Ma'am. You are a royal, and you must never mix with us. We know our place—and we expect you to know yours."[62] Diana returned to her rooms and felt more lonely than ever.

The royal family: (clockwise from left) Queen Elizabeth II, Prince Charles, Prince Phillip, the Queen Mother, Diana (with Prince William).

Diana confessed to a royal servant her feelings about her new mother-in-law, Queen Elizabeth II:

> I'm absolutely petrified of the Queen. I shake all over when I'm in her presence. I can't look her in the eye, and just go to pieces whenever she comes into the room. She tries to be nice and put me at my ease, but I am so embarrassed when I am with her.[63]

Diana also felt that no one ever gave her credit for the work she did. One of Diana's closest friends, Lady Elsa Bowker, said, "She resented that she was never encouraged by the royal family or anyone. She was shy inside and cried for one hour before every function."[64]

In 1991 Diana wrote about how she tried to handle the lack of praise: "I do as I'm expected. What they say behind my back is none of my business, but I come back here [to my bedroom] and I know when I turn my light off at night, I did my best." [65]

The royal family had also begun to grow concerned about what Diana said when she was in public. Although she was representing the royal family on her visits to hospitals and care centers, her strong opinions on issues such as caring for people dependent on alcohol or drugs at times clashed with the beliefs of the royal family.

After a while, Diana was instructed not to make any public statements except those approved beforehand by the palace. She was also told not to give any private interviews to reporters. Diana felt confined because her direct contact with the press was then restricted and she could no longer be herself with the media. The princess began to call herself the "PoW, or Prisoner of Wales." [66]

Diana felt more alone than ever, as she wrote in her biography notes: "There's no better way to dismantle a personality than to isolate it. I was isolated." [67]

Meanwhile, as Charles began to doubt Diana's intelligence, she wondered about what she perceived to be a lack of caring in him. This came about in 1991 when William, who was then nine years old, suffered a severe head injury when a classmate at Ludgrove School accidentally hit him in the head with a golf club.

The royal parents rushed to the hospital where their son had been taken. A neurosurgeon said William had suffered a depressed fracture of his skull. Surgery to relieve pressure on his brain was then performed. But afterward there were concerns that the boy's blood pressure could go up dangerously high and be life threatening. Diana remained at her son's bedside all night, holding his hand and hoping and praying for his recovery. Charles, however, was confident of his son's recovery, so he kept a previously planned engagement by attending an opera.

Uncertain Feelings

In the early days of their marriage, the royal couple seemed to be very happy. Princess Diana was seen squeezing her husband's hand and gazing at him adoringly. Prince Charles, who was normally restrained, also looked as if he were in love with his wife.

But while Charles had wondered early on if he had chosen the right woman to be his wife, Diana also had apprehensions about marrying Charles. She began to have doubts that he loved her; in fact, she suspected that he loved another woman. She later revealed that those doubts were what caused her to falter as she walked down the church aisle.

The woman in question was Camilla Parker-Bowles, who had been one of Charles's close friends since the early 1970s. Diana had suspected that Charles had been in love before he proposed to her, but she did not know who the other woman was until after their engagement.

Charles' relationship with Camilla Parker-Bowles became a point of contention between him and Diana.

During their engagement, Diana thought that Charles was too sympathetic about how distressed Parker-Bowles was by the constant attention of reporters and photographers.

> Whenever he rang me up he said: "Poor Camilla Parker-Bowles. I've had her on the telephone tonight and she says there's lots of press at [her home]. She's having a very rough time."

> I never complained about the press to him because I didn't think it was my position to do so. I asked him: "How many press are out there?" He said, "At least four." I thought, "My God, there's thirty-four here!," and I never told him.[68]

While planning their wedding, Charles gave Diana reason to be suspicious of his feelings toward Parker-Bowles, even though by then Camilla had married and had a son. Charles was about to leave on a lengthy trip to Australia and New Zealand, and Diana knew how badly she would miss him. While talking with him in the study at Kensington Palace, the telephone rang. "It was Camilla, just before he was going for five weeks," Diana later recalled. "I thought, 'Shall I be nice or shall I just sit here?' So I thought I'd be nice so I left them to it [to say good-bye to each other]. It just broke my heart."[69]

Two weeks before her wedding, Diana learned that Charles had given Parker-Bowles a bracelet with the initials *G* and *F* entwined in it. She later learned that *Gladys* and *Fred* were Parker-Bowles's and Charles's secret pet names for each other.

Diana was so distressed that she told her sisters, "I can't marry him. I can't do this. This is absolutely unbelievable." They responded, "Well, bad luck, Duch. . . . You're too late to chicken out."[70]

At the rehearsal three days before her wedding, Diana tried to forget her broken heart. As she later recalled, "I remember being so in love with my [future] husband that I couldn't take my eyes off him. I just absolutely thought I was the luckiest girl in the world. He was going to look after me. Well, I was wrong on that assumption."[71]

Diana later wrote about her wedding,

> I don't think I was happy. . . . The Camilla thing rearing
> its head the whole way through our engagement. . . . I was
> desperately trying to be mature about the situation, but I
> didn't have the foundations to do it, and I couldn't talk to
> anyone about it. . . . There was the big question mark in
> my mind. I realized I had taken on an enormous role, but
> had no idea what I was going into—but *no* idea.[72]

*Throughout their engagement, Diana suspected that Charles was still in
love with another woman.*

Diana again sensed her husband's continued affection for Parker-Bowles on their honeymoon. At a formal dinner for Egypt's President Anwar Sadat, Diana noticed that Charles wore cufflinks with two *C*'s entwined. "Camilla gave you those, didn't she?" Diana asked him. "Yes, so what's wrong? They're a present from a friend." [73] Diana thought it was very indiscreet of him to wear another woman's present on his honeymoon.

Charles and Camilla Parker-Bowles remained close friends after they both married other people. She became a frequent visitor at Charles's house at Highgrove, where she hosted lunches and dinners for Charles and virtually ran his house. In 1991 Diana remained at their home in London when Charles went on a week-long painting holiday in Italy, and Parker-Bowles joined him there.

In an interview after their divorce, Diana recalled that she and Charles "had discussions about Camilla. I once heard him on the telephone in his bath on a hand-held set saying [to Camilla], 'Whatever happens, I will always love you.' I told him afterwards that I had listened at the door, and we had a filthy row." [74]

Diana felt helpless because of her husband's relations with Parker-Bowles. "I wasn't in a position to do anything about it," [75] she said, because her husband was the future king, and she could not help the fact that he was still in love with Parker-Bowles.

Eating Troubles

Charles's suspected affair with Parker-Bowles caused Diana to become physically ill. During this time Diana was suffering from a long-standing eating disorder known as bulimia, or compulsive overeating. When overcome by anxiety or stress—such as that caused by her marital problems—Diana would make herself sick by overeating, then vomit up the food so she would not gain weight. At the height of her eating disorder, she was eating and purging four or five times a day. As she later told an interviewer,

I had bulimia for a number of years. It's like a secret disease. You inflict it upon yourself because your self-esteem is at a low ebb and you don't think you're worthy or valuable. You fill your stomach up four or five times a day—some do it more—and it gives you a feeling of comfort. [76]

According to Diana, her eating troubles began "the week after we got engaged. My husband put his hand on my waistline and said, 'Oh, a bit chubby here, aren't we?' That triggered off something in me."[77]

As the years went by, the troubles in Charles and Diana's marriage continued to grow.

Diana's Eating Disorder

Princess Diana suffered from bulimia, an eating disorder that mainly affects females. Bulimics go on eating binges, and then they try to avoid putting on unwanted pounds by self-induced vomiting.

In his book *Diana: Her True Story*, Andrew Morton describes the characteristics of bulimics—a description that fit Diana quite well.

> Bulimia survives by disguise. It is a sophisticated illness in as much as sufferers do not admit that they have a problem. They always appear to be happy and spend their lives trying to help others. Yet there is rage beneath the sunny smile, anger which sufferers are afraid to express.

> While the roots of bulimia lie in childhood and a disordered family background, uncertainty and anxiety in adult life provide the trigger for the illness. For Diana, [she had been on] an emotional rollercoaster as she had tried to come to terms with her new life as a public figure and the suffocating publicity, as well as her husband's ambiguous behavior towards her.

Stresses that included Camilla Parker-Bowles made Diana ill even before her wedding. "I had a very bad fit of bulimia the night before," she recalled. She later explained that it was brought on by anxieties over the responsibilities she would face as Charles's wife and also from suspicions that he still loved Parker-Bowles. "I ate everything I could possibly find. . . . I was sick as a parrot that night."[78]

However, Diana said she felt "very calm the next morning. I felt I was a lamb to the slaughter. I knew it and couldn't do anything about it."[79]

Anxieties about her rival for her husband's affections swept over Diana again a few hours later as her wedding ceremony began in St. Paul's Cathedral. "Walking down the aisle I spotted Camilla, pale gray (dress), veiled pillbox hat, saw it all, her son Tom standing on a chair."[80]

Diana's binge eating continued on her honeymoon. Aboard the *Britannia,* she would creep into the galley, or kitchen, at odd hours to consume large bowls of ice cream and other treats. As she later wrote,

> By then the bulimia was appalling. It was rife, four times a day on the yacht. Anything I could find I would gobble up

and be sick two minutes later—very tired. So, of course, that slightly got the mood swings going in the sense that one minute one would be happy, next blubbing one's eyes out.[81]

Diana's eating disorder continued throughout her marriage, as she worried about putting on weight that would displease her husband. But she believed that it stemmed from a combination of things: childhood anxieties from feeling unwanted because she was born a girl instead of a boy, the trauma from her parents' divorce, and overattention from the media. Most of all, she believed it came from a lifelong lack of self-esteem that was intensified by not feeling wanted or loved by her husband and, as she later wrote, "the Camilla thing. I was desperate, desperate."[82]

Other Marriage Troubles

Trouble in Diana's marriage to Charles was not confined to Camilla Parker-Bowles; it also concerned their sons. The couple had different parenting styles. Charles not only wanted the boys to be looked after by nannies but also to attend the same schools that he had. Diana, however, insisted on rearing them herself and sending them to public schools.

According to Diana, Charles also had hoped that their second child would be a girl. The princess claimed that when Harry was born, the prince remarked with mild disappointment, "Oh God, it's a boy,"[83] and went off to play polo.

Despite his initial reaction to Harry, however, Charles was thrilled with his new son. But Harry's birth did not improve the royal marriage. Charles's reaction had reminded Diana of how unhappy she had been that her father had wished for a boy. She later said in an interview, "Something inside me closed off. By then I knew he had gone back to his lady, but somehow we'd managed to have Harry. Then suddenly as Harry was born, it just went bang, our marriage, the whole thing went down the drain."[84]

As Diana's self-confidence and popularity grew, Charles reportedly began to be more critical of her. He is said to have begun finding flaws in her personality and behavior, and he even began cracking jokes about a lack of intelligence in her.

Opinions on how to raise their children were another point of contention between Charles and Diana.

Friends and Lovers

During their strained marriage, Charles was not the only one who found comfort in friends and lovers. Although he was frequently seen with just one female friend, Camilla Parker-Bowles, Diana had several relationships with handsome young bachelors.

In 1986 she began a two-year relationship with a London banker that continued until he married. During 1987 Diana also had a close friendship with a major in the Household Cavalry who escorted her to disco dances and rock concerts. In 1991 Diana began a more serious relationship with handsome army major James Hewitt, who gave her riding lessons. These and other relationships were frequently photographed and made the front pages of London's newspapers. If Prince Charles was aware of his wife's relationships with other men, he kept silent about it.

Despite Diana's relationships with a few men, her closest friends were her former apartment roommates and Sarah Ferguson, who worked in a London art house. Red-haired, fun-loving "Fergie," as she came to be known, was the daughter of

Prince Charles's polo master and would soon become Prince Andrew's wife. Both women liked to have a good time and had several other things in common. When Fergie was thirteen, her mother had also walked out of her marriage and her father had also remarried. The two friends shared similar childhoods strained by divorce.

"The arrival of Fergie into the royal circle was a mixed blessing for the Princess," Penny Junor writes.

> On the one hand she was someone closer to her own age and an ally. But she was also a rival. She was . . . undaunted by protocol, relaxed, irreverent and determined to have fun; people talked about her being a breath of fresh air. Diana, who had never been confident at the best of times, felt doubly insecure. As she later admitted, "I got terribly jealous."[85]

Through her friendship with Diana, Fergie met Charles's brother, handsome, fun-loving Prince Andrew. Royal observers said it was love at first sight, and after a brief courtship, the two became engaged.

Diana and Fergie enjoyed getting into playful mischief. Their first of many stunts together was to try to crash Andrew's bachelor party disguised as uniformed policewomen. When they were recognized and turned away, they wore their uniforms to a fashionable nightclub instead.

Their pranks were not popular with the royal family. After one such escapade, Charles reportedly scolded Diana for "trashing the dignity of the royal family." Diana, in turn, chided him for being "stuffy, boring, and old before his time."[86]

The marriage of Sarah Ferguson and Prince Andrew only lasted five years; they divorced in 1992.

Chapter 5

The End of a Fairy Tale

AS HER MARRIAGE was failing, Diana felt she needed to defend herself to those who said she was emotionally unstable. A resulting book, *Diana: Her True Story,* publicly exposed her private anxieties. This resulted in an exchange of television interviews in which both she and Charles admitted that they had been unfaithful to each other. Because of the scandals, the queen agreed that they should separate, which then led to a divorce.

Public Revelations

Diana felt misunderstood and powerless, and she wanted the world to know the reasons for her emotional distress and how trapped she felt in her marriage. She thought this could be done by having a book published, but she did not, however, want to make it appear as if she wrote or authorized such a book. She decided to enlist the aid of a trusted biographer, Andrew Morton, who would write a book in which she would secretly reveal the causes of her anxieties. Morton was instructed to say that Diana had not granted him interviews and that he received his most personal material about Diana from other sources whom he would not disclose.

Diana: Her True Story caused a sensation when it was published in June 1992 and simultaneously serialized in the *Sunday Times.* It revealed Diana's bulimia, suicide attempts because of her unhappy marriage, accusations that Charles was indifferent to her, and her feelings that she was trapped in a loveless marriage and that the royal family and the royal court were cold to and disapproved of her. Most damaging, the book revealed that Prince Charles's love for Camilla Parker-Bowles continued after his marriage to Diana. That, together with pressures of being the Princess of Wales and harassment from the media, drove her to attempt suicide five times. Diana said the attempts were cries for help rather than serious efforts to end her life.

The royal family was shocked that Diana had gone public with her anxieties and accusations. She denied having had anything to do with the book, including granting interviews with Morton that appeared in it. Morton kept Diana's secret that she had in fact given him audio tape recordings in answer to his questions.

Years later, in disclosing Diana's total cooperation in the book, Morton said that to disguise her role in it, he attributed quotes she gave him to "a close friend," or if he used her direct quote, he disguised it by saying "she told friends." He revealed that the book was "to all intents and purposes her autobiography. There were 4,000 of her words in the book. She approved it, including her first-person speech. [She also] made a number of alterations of fact and emphasis."[87]

As soon as the book became talked about, Diana regretted having actually given secretly written interviews to Morton. She feared that she would never be forgiven for the revelations in the

Diana the Psychic

Throughout her life, Diana had several premonitions of illnesses and disasters and considered herself able to predict the future. When she suffered from her eating disorder and her marriage was in trouble, she consulted astrologers and spiritualists.

Diana explained the psychic side of her nature in Andrew Morton's *Diana: Her True Story*, adding that she believed that her deceased paternal grandmother, Countess Cynthia Spencer, protected her.

She looks after me in the spirit world. I know that for a fact. Used to stay at Park house with us [before her death.] She was sweet and wonderful and special. Divine, really.

I'd never discuss it with anyone, they would all think I was a nut. I used the word "psychic" to my policemen a couple of times and they have freaked out. I've got a lot of [déjà vu]. Places I think I've been before, people I've met.

book. "It was a great mistake," she told a trusted friend, Lord Palumbo. "I really regret it."[88]

Because of the scandalous revelations in the book and the media's coverage of the obvious coldness between Diana and Charles during their royal visit to South Korea that November, the queen summoned them to Buckingham Palace. In what later was described as an informal talk over tea, Queen Elizabeth cautioned them about the dangers of their failing marriage and reminded them that divorce could not be considered, even for a moment.

Views on a Failed Marriage

A British ambassador who knew Charles and Diana since they first started to date later commented on their troubled marriage:

The widening gulf in their marriage was clearly evident during Charles and Diana's trip to South Korea in November 1992.

It is sad, but it was all wrong from the very beginning. To Diana, Charles was a fantasy figure with whom she was besotted [infatuated]; to Charles, Diana was the young bride who would become the perfect princess, always at his side and willing to fall in with his wishes and his lifestyle.[89]

Charles's and Diana's differences were apparent to Penny Junor as she followed the lives of the British monarchy:

There was never any depth to the relationship or to their understanding of each other. Diana couldn't be the soul mate he wanted in a wife. She didn't share his enthusiasm for books or horses or gardening, or opera or any of the dozens of things which she had pretended to be so interested in at the onset. She was not the one to cure the loneliness and uncertainty of his life, or to give him the unconditional love and support and reassurance he needed to make him a confident and happy man—because she desperately needed all of those things herself.[90]

Another "royal watcher" had a different view of why the marriage was breaking up:

The problems of the marriage have come out in the open because Di's self-confidence has developed. She now appreciates her own incredible sexuality and the fact that the world is at her feet. This adoration used to terrify her. Now she quite enjoys the effect she has."[91]

The personal revelations in Morton's book about Diana and her anxieties distressed Charles greatly, but they also tended to validate his suspicions that she was emotionally unstable.

A Wake-Up Call

After Diana publicly revealed her bulimia problem through the Morton book, she set about trying to do something to end her eating disorder. She did this by seeing doctors and psychologists, also at her husband's urging. They prescribed Prozac, an antidepressant drug, which she then took for several years.

Medication, along with getting a firmer grasp on her life, helped bring her bulimia under control.

"I think the bulimia actually woke me up," Diana wrote in 1991. "I hated myself so much I didn't think I was good enough. I thought I wasn't good enough for Charles, I wasn't a good enough mother—I mean doubts as long as one's leg. . . . I suddenly realized what I was going to lose if I let go, and was it worth it?"[92]

Diana's strategy for winning her battle with bulimia was threefold. It involved exercise, times with good friends, and a sensible dietary plan aimed at eating for good health and no other reason.

Separation

On December 3, 1992, Diana visited her sons at Ludgrove, their boarding school, and told them she and their father were going to separate. But, she added, that while agreeing to a separation, she did not want a divorce from him.

William, then ten, had been aware of his father's attentions to Camilla Parker-Bowles. As Diana later explained,

> I put it to William, particularly, that if you find someone you love in life, you must hang on to it and look after it, and if you were lucky enough to find someone who loved you, then one must protect it.
>
> William asked me what had been going on and could I answer his questions, which I did. He said, "Was that the reason why our marriage had broken up?" and I said, "Well, there were three of us in this marriage, and the pressure of the media was another factor, so the two together were very difficult, that although I still loved Papa, I couldn't live under the same roof as him, and likewise with him. . . ." I put it gently, without resentment or any anger.[93]

Six days later, on December 9, Prime Minister John Major formally announced to Parliament that the Prince and Princess of Wales were separating amicably, but had no plans to divorce.

One of Diana's friends wrote in her diary about how both Diana and Charles accepted the separation:

> Diana and Charles agreed they were incompatible and decided on a parting of the ways. She could see a glimmer of light. Relief that reality of the situation seemed to be faced. . . . First time Diana slept through night without sleeping pills. Gained enormous strength. Diana phones to say that he agrees [to a separation]. She is elated and can sleep now.[94]

Members of the media exploited the royal couple's separation in a barrage of newspaper, magazine, and television stories. They speculated on everything from Diana being crazy and suicidal to Charles never having loved her in the first place.

As 1992 drew to a close, Queen Elizabeth spoke of the separation and the media attention it received in her annual national television greeting on November 20. Earlier that year, the marriage of Prince Andrew and Sarah Ferguson had ended, and

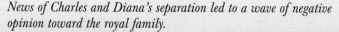

News of Charles and Diana's separation led to a wave of negative opinion toward the royal family.

Windsor Castle nearly burned to the ground in an accidental fire. The queen called it an *annus horribilis,* or a "horrible year."

Royal Revelations

It had also been a horrible year for Prince Charles and Princess Diana. Their separation did not improve their marriage, and they began to publicly criticize each other and reveal more marital difficulties. It resulted in a public bickering match or royal duel that drove them further apart.

On December 3, 1993, Diana announced that, because she could no longer tolerate media pressure, she was seeking a more private life. She would reduce her public and official duties.

Charles kept a low profile too, but only for a while. He remained silent about accusations of his unfaithfulness in Morton's book until he felt he had to explain his side to the public. He did this when he was interviewed on British television by Jonathan Dimbleby.

In the interview, Dimbleby asked Charles about allegations that he had been "persistently unfaithful" to Diana "from the beginning" of their marriage. Charles replied, "There is no truth in so much of this speculation."[95]

Without mentioning her by name, he added that the woman with whom he was said to have had a longtime affair was "a great friend. . . . She has been a friend for a very long time . . . and will be a friend for a very long time."[96]

Next, Dimbleby asked a very sensitive question: "Did you try to be faithful and honorable to your wife when you took on the vow of marriage?" "Yes," Charles replied. "And you were?" Dimbleby asked. "Yes," Charles said, then added, "until it became irretrievably broken down, us both having tried."[97]

Charles then explained how he personally felt. He said the breakdown of his marriage was "deeply regrettable" and "a dreadful thing" that had caused "a certain amount of damage."[98]

In the same interview, Charles alluded to Diana not fitting into the royal life, but he did not identify her by name, saying,

> I do think those people who marry into my family find
> it increasingly difficult to do so because of all the added

pressure. . . . Because of suddenly finding that they're put into positions for which they are simply not trained, and the strains and stresses of that become, in some cases, almost intolerable.[99]

After the interview, when reporters pressed Dimbleby for the name of the woman with whom Prince Charles had been unfaithful, Dimbleby replied, "The clear context was that we were talking about Camilla Parker-Bowles."[100] He added that Charles said his marriage broke down after five years, in 1986.

Charles's admitted infidelity further distressed his mother, the queen, and it shocked even Diana's detractors.

Morton's revealing book and Charles's televised interview were vast public departures from the royal family's tradition of keeping its personal problems private. As the London *Sunday Times* commented, "The royals are not 'allowed' to have personal problems."[101] Diana and Charles had broken the rules by making theirs public.

Just as the scandal of Charles's admitted infidelity began to subside, a new book surfaced that revealed Diana's unfaithfulness. Anna Pasternak's book *Princess in Love,* which was published in September 1994, claimed that during her marriage and separation, Diana had carried on a five-year affair with cavalry officer captain James Hewitt.

Diana feared that some people might not understand that she had turned to Hewitt for comfort and affection because of her husband's infidelity. She also felt betrayed by Hewitt because he had helped write the revealing book. As she later said, "He was a great friend of mine at a very difficult time. I was absolutely devastated when this book appeared because I had trusted him."[102]

After publication of *Princess in Love,* Diana felt she needed to publicly defend her affair with Hewitt, so she granted her first solo television interview. In a BBC *Panorama* television broadcast on November 20, 1995, that was watched by 21.1 million people worldwide, Diana confirmed her affair with Hewitt. She admitted, "Yes, I was in love with him."[103]

However, despite her marital unhappiness because, as she said, "there were three of us in the marriage, so it was a bit crowded,"[104] she again said that she did not want a divorce.

Feeling the need to tell her side of the story, Diana agreed to a television interview with the BBC's Panorama *in 1995.*

Diana's interview won the sympathy and affection of millions of television viewers, but it horrified the queen, who had not been notified beforehand. The queen may have been most upset by Diana's criticism of the monarchy, when Diana said, "I would like a monarchy that has more contact with its people. I don't mean riding bicycles, but having a more in-depth understanding." [105]

When asked if she thought she would become queen, Diana's reply may also have unsettled Queen Elizabeth: "No, I don't. I'd like to be a queen of people's hearts. But I don't see myself as queen of this country." [106]

Divorce

Believing by then that no chance of a reconciliation was possible and that the public scandal was a threat to the image and stability of the monarchy, Queen Elizabeth sent Prince Charles a letter in December. She said it was "highly desirable" [107] that he and Diana divorce, and quickly.

With reasons that Diana would not publicly reveal, she hesitated to agree to the divorce until February 28, 1996. Months of negotiations concerning the terms of the divorce settlement followed. When the terms were mutually agreed upon on July 12, 1996, Charles and Diana announced their decision to divorce.

Debate was rampant regarding why the royal couple was divorcing. Their problems began, Penny Junor says in her book *Charles: Victim or Villain?* with the difficult task he had in choosing a wife in the first place:

> The [royal] system required the Prince to find a wife and produce an heir, but not just any wife—a wife who was a member of the Church of England, who was pure, with no past experience of men, who was well-bred and who understood the protocol and would be able to share the duties of monarchy. The criteria were unrealistic for the 1980s.
>
> If the system orchestrated an inevitably disastrous marriage, the perception that the Prince was responsible for it came from the media, which the Princess used unscrupulously in the war against her husband. The public fell in love with a Princess of Wales that the newspapers created. [108]

Diana's Self-Confidence

In a BBC *Panorama* television interview on November 20, 1995, Diana assessed what her inner strengths meant to the monarchy.

> I think every strong woman in history has had to walk down a similar path [as I]. I think it's [my] strength that causes the confusion and the fear [in the royal family]. [They wonder] Why is she strong? Where does she get it from? Where is she taking it? Where is she going to use it? Why does the public still support her?

Some of Prince Charles's friends blamed Diana for the deterioration of their marriage, hinting publicly that she was mentally unstable. Diana was suspicious that the royal family encouraged the rumors and began to fear that she might be committed to a mental institution.

However, Diana may well have been mistaken about this. According to Junor, "There was no campaign to discredit Diana. In fact, [Charles] had given specific instructions to his staff to say and do nothing to reflect badly upon Diana." [109]

Under the terms of the divorce, Diana would remain living at Kensington Palace and be known as Diana, Princess of Wales. But she lost the prefix HRH ("Her Royal Highness") from her title and the right to ascend to the British throne.

Even after her divorce, members of the press continued to follow Diana's every move.

The divorce settlement was financially generous to Diana. She could keep all of her jewelry and would receive a one-time alimony settlement of nearly $23 million as well as a generous monthly allowance. Of greatest importance to Diana, however, was that she would be involved in all decisions about her sons and would share custody of them with Charles.

Diana hoped the media's interest in her would wane after her divorce, but it did not. While Charles escaped the media by retreating to his garden outside London or to the hunting fields of Scotland, Diana was harassed daily by reporters and photographers.

Photographers pursued Diana not only to record her daily activities but also any meeting she might have with a new love. One even promised, with a wink, that he and his telephoto lens would "follow Diana to the grave."[110] Sadly, it was to become a prophetic threat.

Chapter 6

The People's Princess

AFTER HER DIVORCE from Prince Charles, Diana blossomed as a more confident, independent woman. She found a new purpose in life as an unofficial British ambassador for controversial humanitarian causes. While carrying on these crusades, which made her very popular with the public and the media, Diana fell in love again.

Just as Diana had appeared to have found new confidence and happiness, she was killed in a car crash. Millions of people around the world mourned the loss of "the People's Princess."

Royalty and commoners eulogized Diana, who left a legacy of caring that some predicted would have a profound effect on the British monarchy. Biographers, however, were unable to fathom who she really was, and Princess Diana has become one of the most enigmatic figures of the twentieth century.

A New Diana

Diana became like a new person after her divorce. She gained a new self-confidence that others noticed.

"She managed to regain that strength I knew she had and which she knew she had," said one of Diana's friends, Diana Donovan. "She could see the affects she was having on her own and that people were starting to believe in her. As a result, she was starting to believe in herself."[111]

A great part of Diana's new self-confidence came from her continued involvement in humanitarian causes. In fact, early in 1997, only months before her death, Diana sought government advice on how she might be of help to her country, saying,

> I'd like to be an ambassador for this country to every country in the world. I'd like to represent this country

abroad in the best way possible—by showing the essential tolerance and concern that is the best of England, the best of any people.[112]

British prime minister Tony Blair approved, saying, "I think it is very important that Princess Diana is allowed to carry on the work that she is doing. She earns a lot of respect and admiration from people all around the world. I'm very happy for that to continue." [113]

Diana's constant humanitarian work throughout the world earned her the respect and admiration of millions.

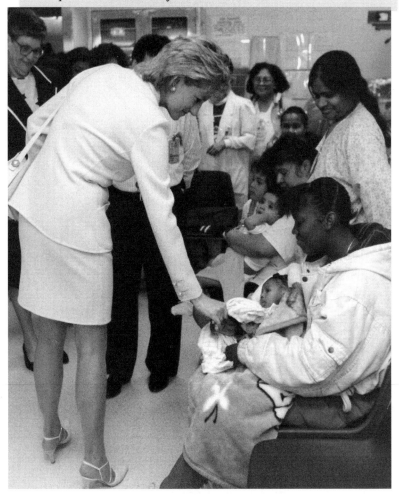

However, no firm arrangement was made for Diana to become an official ambassador of goodwill for Britain. Undaunted, she assumed the task on an unofficial basis.

A Visit to Chicago

Among her appearances at humanitarian causes after her divorce, Diana visited Chicago to raise money for cancer research. It was her first engagement as a self-styled "Queen of Hearts." Besides dining and dancing at events scheduled by her city hosts, she visited Cook County Hospital, where she cradled an infant who was close to death, visited other children suffering from cancer, and she sat with a man who had been paralyzed in a gun battle. She left the hospital with tears in her eyes.

Diana's visit had a profound effect on the hospital's patients and doctors. Dr. William Hayden, director of Pediatric Critical Care, said,

> People ask what good such a visit can possibly do. Well, I saw a lot of smiles from patients. [Diana] exudes intelligence, her questions were sharp, her eye contact real, her emotions readable and appropriate, and her smile heartwarming. How much better does it have to be?[114]

Jane Fincher, a photographer who frequently photographed Diana on her visits to hospitals, recalled that "she would walk into a [hospital] room and there would be a special chair for her. Instead of sitting in [it] she'd sit on the bed of the person she was visiting, or on the floor."[115]

Seeking a More Private Life

Diana was visibly changed after her divorce. As her best friend, Lady Rosa Monckton, said at the time, "She's living her life as she wants to live it, and she's free of the restrictions she had before. You can see that in the way she looks. She's much happier with herself, and she's more calm."[116]

One of the changes that Diana had made was to cut back on her public appearances so that she could live a more private life. Diana told the media,

When I started my public life twelve years ago, I understood that the media might be interested in what I did. I realized then that their attention would inevitably focus on both our private and public lives. But I was not aware of how overwhelming that attention would become; nor the extent to which it would affect my public duties and my personal life, in a manner that has been hard to bear.[117]

Diana said she would continue to support a small number of charities, but she added, "My first priority will continue to be our children, William and Harry, who deserve as much love, care and attention as I am able to give, as well as an appreciation of the tradition into which they were born."[118]

Diana also made it perfectly clear that she would raise her sons as good royals: "Once or twice, I've heard people say that Diana's out to destroy the monarchy, which has me bewildered. Why would I want to destroy something that is my children's future?"[119]

A New Cause

Early in 1997 Diana took up a new humanitarian cause that became a virtual crusade for her. She learned that about 100 million

Dealing with Attention

At first, Diana was overwhelmed not only by the attention she received from reporters and photographers but also from the public. She said that she learned later, after her divorce, how to handle this, as she explained in Andrew Morton's book *Diana: Her True Story.*

> The size of the crowds—if that doesn't make me seem like a pop star; people thanking me for bringing happiness in their lives. . . . Thanking for coming; thank-you for making the effort; thank-you for being you and all those things, [I] never used to believe.

> Now I'm more comfortable receiving that sort of information whether or not it's true. I can now digest that sort of thing, whereas I used to throw it back. No-one has ever said to me "Well done." Because I had a smile on my face, everybody thought I was having a wonderful time. That's what they chose to think—it made them happier thinking that.

personal land mines, bomblike explosives buried in the ground, had been scattered across sixty countries during wartime to explode on enemy soldiers. But many of these mines remained hidden in the earth after wars. About every fifteen minutes, an innocent person, sometimes a child, accidentally steps on a land mine and is either killed or suffers terrible injuries, including loss of limbs.

In an effort to raise awareness about land mines, Diana visits with Sandra Thijica (on lap) and other land mine victims in Angola.

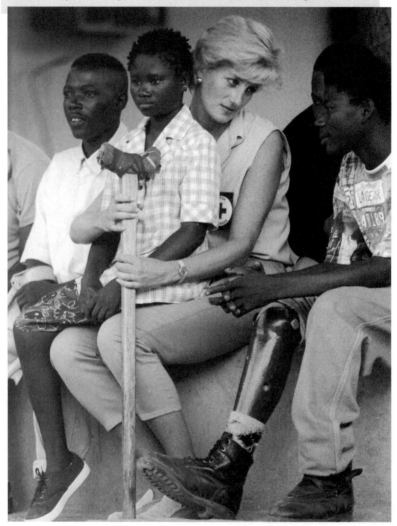

In January 1997 Diana went to Africa as a guest of the Red Cross to bring world attention to the use of land mines and raise awareness about their victims. She visited Angola, a nation where thousands of people had been killed in a civil war a few years earlier. After the war, people were still being injured or killed from personal land mines that remained buried in the ground.

Diana commented on her trip: "My purpose was to draw world attention to this vital, prohibitive, largely neglected issue."[120]

Photographs of Diana walking across a minefield to demonstrate the danger of personal land mines brought the horror home to the world. After seeing the photographs, one of Diana's close friends, Lady Elsa Bowker asked, "Aren't you frightened?" Diana replied, "I'm never frightened when I'm doing good."[121]

The Summer of 1997

Despite a public assertion that she was going to cut back on public appearances, Diana kept busy with humanitarian work during the summer of 1997.

In June, Diana attended a seven-thousand-dollar-a-plate fundraising dinner in Washington, D.C., during which she said, "In the name of humanity, ban land mines and make the world a safer place."[122]

At her son William's suggestion, on June 25, 1997, Diana gave away seventy-nine of her dresses and gowns for a charity auction at Christy's in New York City. The sale raised over $3.26 million for AIDS and cancer research.

That August, Diana visited war-torn Bosnia in Eastern Europe to further work toward eliminating land mines. She spent several fifteen-hour days visiting victims, including a boy who lost both of his feet from an exploding mine. Again, photos of Diana with land-mine victims made the front pages of newspapers around the world to help her in her crusade to urge governments everywhere to ban the deployment of land mines.

During that summer, said Diana's friend Sally Quinn, who was a *Washington Post* reporter, there was an incredible sense of irony about [Diana], her image and her publicity. She didn't seem at all angry about the press. On the contrary, she was what I would call accepting. I asked her how she withstood the lack of privacy and the unbelievable media interest in her. She smiled and shrugged and said something to the effect of "what will be, will be." [I felt Diana] had actually discovered who she really was.[123]

Summer Love

The summer of 1997 brought a new man into Diana's life. Through her father's friendship with Egyptian multimillionaire Mohamed Al Fayed, Diana came to know his son, Emad "Dodi" Fayed, and the media soon reported that they were in love. Forty-two-year-old Dodi Fayed was Egyptian but was now living in London, where his wealthy father conducted a worldwide oil business and was generous to charitable causes.

Fayed was considered a jet-set playboy who coproduced or cofinanced several movies, including *Chariots of Fire* and *Hook*. He had been previously married, for only eight months, to model Suzanne Gregard. His father had introduced him to Diana in 1986 when Dodi was playing in a polo match against her then-husband, Prince Charles.

Through the years, Diana had sometimes accepted invitations to Fayed's parties. In July 1997 she accepted an invitation to take her sons with her aboard Fayed's yacht *Jonikal* off the coast of St. Tropez, France. Fayed joined them on the yacht and ashore at his father's estate at Castel Sainte Helene.

After her divorce from Prince Charles, Diana's relationship with the media, and especially with the paparazzi—that is, the aggressive freelance photographers who took candid photographs of celebrities, became as enigmatic as her true nature. She encouraged the media to follow along on her crusade against land mines to publicize that cause, but she complained when she was photographed with Dodi Fayed, pleading that she had no privacy.

Some critics said that she was manipulating the media, and as reporters and photographers resented being used, they pur-

Diana appeared to be happy once again after beginning a relationship with Dodi Fayed (pictured).

sued her all the more. Her friend Lord Palumbo later said in the Arts and Entertainment television biography *Diana: Her True Story,* "She wanted to use the press on her own terms, and I said it doesn't work like that." [124]

When the media learned that Diana and the princes were aboard Fayed's yacht, boatloads of paparazzi arrived. She was photographed with Fayed, setting off worldwide speculation that she had found a new love. Friends, including supermodel Cindy Crawford, agreed. Crawford later said Diana told her, "Dodi is a fantastic man. He fills me with love and care." [125] Richard Kay, a reporter for the *London Daily Mail,* said Diana told him that she was "blissfully happy" [126] with Fayed.

Only a few years before, Diana had told her exercise trainer, Richard Greene, how she felt about marriage. "I think romance is overstated," she said. "I think now what I really want is someone who can be a lifelong friend." [127]

Dodi Fayed may have been that friend. As Diana's friend Lady Bowker recalled later, "She called me from France. I did not recognize her on the telephone. I told her, 'What a strong voice.' She said, 'I have a strong voice because I have become very strong. I fear nothing.'" [128]

There has been a lot of speculation about the nature of Diana's relationship with Fayed. Some believed that they planned to marry, but others doubted the notion. Whatever

Diana and Her Future

In Andrew Morton's *Diana: Her True Story*, which was published before her separation from Prince Charles, Diana revealed her thoughts for her future.

I think I'm going to cut a very different path from everyone else. I'm going to break away from this set-up [restrictions from the royal family] and go and help the man on the street.... I don't know yet, but I'm being pushed more and more that way.

I don't like the glamorous occasions anymore—I feel uncomfortable with them. I would much rather be doing something with sick people—I'm more comfortable there.

I have been positive about the future for some time, but obviously there's endless question marks, especially when my space is crowded around me. . . . I always felt so different—I felt I was in the wrong shell. I knew my life was going to be a winding road.

I don't want my friends to be hurt and think I've dropped them, but I haven't got time to sit and gossip, I've got things to do and time is precious. . . . Last August a friend said to me that I'm going to marry somebody who's foreign, or who has got a lot of foreign blood in them. I thought it was always interesting. I do know I'm going to remarry or live with someone.

their relationship, Diana seemed happy when they were together.

One of Fayed's friends, Nona Summes, said,

> They were each in love with the fantasy about the other. Both were sweet, but they didn't know what each other was. She made an adorable first impression, but she had intense addictive relationships. Dodi saw himself as the knight on the steed, ready to defend his princess against the *paparazzi*. They were in many ways ill-fated and the perfect awful couple.[129]

Diana's Last Day

On Saturday, August 30, 1997, Diana and Dodi Fayed dined together in Paris at the Espadon restaurant in the Ritz Hotel owned by Fayed's father. At this time, Fayed gave Diana a $285,000 diamond ring which many people later assumed was an engagement ring.

After dinner, hounded by paparazzi, they and Trevor Rees-Jones, a bodyguard employed by the al-Fayeds, got into a Mercedes S280 limousine. Their chauffeur, Henri Paul, shouted to a handful of paparazzi who were snapping pictures of them, "Don't bother following, you won't catch us."[130] But as the limousine sped away, photographers pursued at speeds of seventy to one hundred miles an hour in cars and on motorcycles.

The chase continued into the slightly curving tunnel at the Pont de l'Alma bridge shortly before midnight. Turning the wheel to avoid an approaching car, the driver lost control of the limousine. It crashed into a concrete pillar and became a mangled mess of steel.

Fayed and the driver, Henri Paul, died at the scene of the crash. Diana was taken by ambulance to La Pitie Salpetriere Hospital, where she underwent two hours of emergency surgery for chest injuries that included a torn pulmonary artery. She died of cardiac arrest at 4 A.M. the following morning.

Diana had been unconscious after the crash and felt no pain, according to her mother. "She knew nothing," Frances Shand-Kydd said later. "She did not suffer at all."[131]

Police investigators examine the wreckage at the site of the fatal car accident that took the lives of Diana, Dodi Fayed, and their chauffeur.

After the Accident

When notified of Diana's death, her brother, Charles Spencer, told reporters, "I always believed that the press would kill her in the end. Not even I could imagine that they would take such a direct hand in her death as seems to be the case." [132]

Many others also blamed the paparazzi for Diana's death. However, besides their high-speed chase, police later revealed that Henri Paul, the driver who had died in the crash, was legally intoxicated and also had been taking medication for depression.

When the accident occurred, Prince Charles had been on vacation in Scotland with Princes William, then fifteen, and Harry, twelve. After breaking the sad news to them, he took the boys to church. He then flew to Paris on September 1 with Diana's sisters to accompany Diana's body back to Britain.

Bodyguard Trevor Rees-Jones recovered from his injuries a few weeks after the accident but could not remember details. The following March he told police that he remembered that

Diana was conscious immediately after the crash and called out Dodi Fayed's name.

After the accident, manslaughter and negligence charges were filed against nine photographers and a motorcycle driver who had been chasing the limousine before the fatal crash. However, after a two-year investigation, French authorities dismissed the charges against them. They concluded that the accident had occurred because Henri Paul had driven the fatal car while intoxicated.

"How Lucky They Are"

In a telephone call just six hours before her death, Diana told friend and reporter Richard Kay that she had "decided to radically change her life."[133] They would be the last thoughts Diana shared with anyone who survived her.

Kay later explained Diana's statement: "Millions of women dreamed of changing places with her, but the princess I knew yearned for the ordinary routine of their lives. 'They don't know how lucky they are,' she would say."[134]

Diana was planning to return home to London the next day to join her sons, who were spending the month with their father at Balmoral Castle in Scotland. She would complete her obligations to her charities, and then, in November, she planned to completely withdraw from her formal public life. She was looking forward to finally being able to live not as a celebrity but as a private person.

The World Grieves

Upon learning of Diana's death, Prime Minister Tony Blair told reporters,

> We are today a nation in Great Britain in a state of shock and in grief that is so deeply painful for us. She was a wonderful and warm human being, though her own life was often sadly touched by tragedy. She touched the lives of so many others in Britain and throughout the world with joy and comfort. . . .
>
> People everywhere kept faith with Princess Diana. They liked her. They loved her and regarded here as one of

the people. She was the people's princess, and that is how she will stay and how she will remain in our hearts and our memories forever.[135]

The world mourned for Princess Diana with a great outpouring of love and flowers. London's flower vendors grossed a total of nearly $45 million by selling flowers to mourners, who placed ten thousand tons of bouquets at the gates of St. James's, Kensington, and Buckingham Palaces.

Thousands of people waited in lines for up to eight hours to lay flowers and sign condolence books at St. James's Palace, where Diana's body rested in a private chapel. The mourners frequently proclaimed, "She was one of us."[136]

"Although I didn't know her and had never met her, I feel like I have lost a friend," a woman from New Zealand wrote in one of the condolence books. Another grieving person wrote, "Your life had great meaning to me, your happiness was important to me. I never wanted you to suffer." A third wrote, "Not since JFK [assassinated president John F. Kennedy] has the

The world showed its love for Princess Diana by sending thousands of flowers to Buckingham Palace.

tragic public passing of a vibrant, charismatic life touched the world so deeply."[137]

The Queen Pays Tribute

The royal family was criticized for not appearing to share in the public grieving immediately after Diana's death. Newspaper headlines pleaded with them to "show us you care." Responding to this, Queen Elizabeth II went on live television the day before Diana's funeral and said,

> What I say to you now as your Queen and as a grandmother, I say from my heart. First, I want to pay tribute to Diana, myself. She was an exceptional and gifted human being. In good times and bad, she never lost her capacity to smile and laugh, to inspire others with her warmth and kindness. I admired and respected her for her energy and commitment to others, especially for her devotion to her two boys.
>
> No one who knew Diana will ever forget her. Millions of others who never met her, but felt they knew her, will remember her. I, for one, believe there are lessons to be drawn from her life and from the extraordinary and moving reaction to her death. I share in your determination to cherish her memory.[138]

Diana's Funeral

The funeral procession for Diana began at Kensington Palace on the morning of September 6, 1997. A gun carriage drawn by six black horses carried the solid oak coffin, which was draped in the maroon and gold royal standard and topped by three white wreaths. The flowers were tulips from her son William; roses from son Harry, with a note he wrote saying "Mummy;" and lillies from her brother.

Crowds of people standing twenty deep lined the streets as the funeral proceeded to Buckingham Palace. The queen and members of the royal family stood outside the gates as the procession passed. At St. James's Palace, Prince Charles; his sons,

Royal Guards carry Diana's casket after the funeral services.

William and Harry; his father, Prince Philip; and Diana's brother, Charles Spencer, Earl of Althorp; all began slowly walking a few steps behind the gun carriage. Following them were five representatives from each of the 110 charities that Diana had helped, including Red Cross volunteers, hospice workers, the homeless, orphans and their caregivers, and people with AIDS.

When the funeral procession reached Westminster Abbey, where British kings, statesmen, and poets are buried, two thousand mourners were already in place. Among those who came to pay their final respects were the queen and forty-three members of the royal family and Diana's mother, Frances Shand-Kydd, with her children and grandchildren. Foreign dignitaries included Queen Noor of Jordan, former King Constantine of Greece, and Princess Margaret of the Netherlands. First Lady Hillary Clinton led the American contingent, which included Henry Kissinger and movie notables Tom Cruise, Tom Hanks, and Steven Spielberg. Also attending were opera star Luciano Pavarotti and Diana's longtime friend, singer Elton John.

The archbishop of Canterbury, the Reverend George Carey, spoke a tribute and led a prayer, saying, in part,

> We give thanks to God for Diana, Princess of Wales—for her sense of joy and for the way she gave so much to so many people. . . . Her life touched us all, and we give thanks for those qualities and strengths that endeared her to us. . . . She became a beacon of strength and a source of hope for so many.[139]

Charles Spencer delivered a eulogy that praised his sister's life and suggested that the monarchy learn from her and show more warmth to the people. His words stirred thousands outside the cathedral to applause, which then began by those inside.

A Friend's Tribute

British author Clive James remembered his close friend Diana in a tribute after her death that appeared in the September 15, 1997, issue of the *New Yorker*.

> Even before I met her, I had already guessed she was a handful. After I met her, there was no doubt about it. Clearly on a hair trigger, she was unstable at best, and when the squeeze was on she was a fruitcake on the rampage.
>
> I was even convinced that she would get herself killed, and that conviction made me love her to distraction, as if I had become a small part of some majestic tragic poem. . . . I feared for her as I loved her, and the fear intensified the love. . . . She wasn't just beautiful. She was like the sun coming up: coming up giggling."

After the funeral service in Westminster Abbey, the coffin was driven to the Spencer family estate at Althorp for a private interment. Princess Diana was buried on an island in the center of a small lake, her grave surrounded by trees that she and her sons had planted a few years before. It was a part of the family estate that she had especially loved for its beauty and privacy.

A memorial to Diana was built on the Spencer estate. It includes a museum containing memorabilia from both her personal and public lives. There are also plans to erect another memorial in London, which would be more accessible to the public.

Epilogue

The Enigmatic Princess

BOTH BEFORE AND after Princess Diana's death, a number of biographers tried to understand who she was and the reasons for her sometimes troubled behavior. In 1997 a new biography of Diana suggested that she may have been the victim of a borderline personality disorder that began in childhood and haunted her throughout her life. Whether true or not, it is certain that Diana's emotional problems were greater than most imagined, and she remains a fascinating enigma.

Late in 1999 a newly published book entitled *Diana in Search of Herself*, took a new look at the princess. Its author, Sally Bedell Smith, says the book focuses on exploring the interplay of Diana's character and her temperament. She drew on sources and interviews that other biographers had not used, which led her to conclude that Diana was more emotionally disturbed than most people thought:

> During Diana's lifetime, few were willing to confront directly the extent of her emotional problems. For the first half of her life, when she was usually in a protected environment, Diana managed to keep her problems in check, except for occasional flare-ups when she was in stressful situations. But after the age of nineteen [when she married Charles], Diana was often out of control, her fragile psyche cracking under the strain of public life. [140]

Smith then quotes Dr. Michael Adler, chairman of the National AIDS Trust, who knew Diana from her visits to AIDS patients:

She clearly should have had a lot more professional help. I think she needed rather intense professional counseling and psychological support, and I was never certain that she ever had that in a manner that I would have thought was totally helpful.[141]

According to Smith,

Prince Charles, who witnessed her extreme behavior longer than anyone, lacked the knowledge and temperament to help her deal with her torment. He probably deserves more credit than he has received for trying to get Diana into therapy on several occasions. But his standard responses to her—pleading, giving in, retreating in anger—only seemed to feed her volatility. Perhaps Charles gave up on Diana too quickly, but he did so out of frustration and ignorance, not for lack of concern.[142]

The outpouring of grief after her death left no doubt that Diana was loved by the world.

Diana's friends and family tended to minimize her emotional problems or focused on her warmth, wit, and other qualities, ignoring her signs of depression. Her media adviser, Jane Atkinson, said she believed the "real" Diana was "withdrawn and detached. The effort she made to come out of that state of mind was considerable. The real Diana was a more brooding person."[143]

"By denying the extent of her difficulties, everyone around Diana enabled her to stay on a self-destructive path," claims Smith. "The press played an especially damaging role by building her up one minute and knocking her down the next."[144]

In her book Smith says that Diana may have suffered from borderline personality disorder. Borderline personalities feel inferior and dependent and are typically confused about their identity. They are self-destructive, easily depressed, panicky, and volatile. But on the surface they are apt to be charming, insightful, witty, and lively. [They can] appear 'superficially intact' while experiencing 'dramatic internal chaos.' "[145]

Smith's research also points out a connection between people with borderline personality disorders and those suffering from bulimia:

> The comfort Diana sought from bulimic bingeing and purging was also an example of the impulsive behavior characteristic of a borderline [personality]. A number of studies have shown that as many as a third of bulimics suffer from the borderline personality disorder. Diana's well-documented suicidal gestures and threats were related forms of impulsiveness consistent with the disorder.[146]

Jonathan Dimbleby also writes of Diana's emotional problems in his book *The Prince of Wales:*

> Whatever clinical or psychiatric label was appropriate to the Princess's distress, its effect on her marriage to the Prince could hardly be in doubt. Her extreme swings of mood from depression to rage; her overwhelming feelings of boredom, loneliness and emptiness, futility and abandonment; her lack of self-image or, as she expressed

it to friends, her feeling that she did not know who she really was; the intense emotional pain that she must have endured in those years; all were bound to place a terrible strain on a marriage which was already subject to external pressures that no other relationship in the land had to experience.[147]

Smith says that while one cannot say with certainty that Diana had a borderline personality disorder, the evidence is compelling. As Smith explains, Diana talked about a sense of destiny—

her need to achieve good by fulfilling a role she had trouble defining. Although her identity was fractured, she kept to her quest and seized opportunities to do her bit for society. But Diana couldn't sustain her good works for the simple reason that her own problems consumed so much of her time and energy. Yet, given the extent to which Diana was ruled by her inconstant emotions, the wonder is that she accomplished as much as she did.[148]

"It may ultimately be impossible to fully explain Diana because she was so mercurial," Smith concludes. "Even those close to her had trouble grasping what was going on in her mind."[149]

Princess Diana's Legacy

Diana's struggle in life and her tragic death left behind some unfinished business that would be her legacy to her country and the world.

For one thing, Diana's experiences with the media prompted her to campaign for privacy rights. In life, she failed to get a British law enacted that would protect the privacy of public figures such as herself. In death, according to Geoffrey Robertson, a leading British civil-rights lawyer, she may have a greater influence in the matter:

Diana was killed fleeing the flashbulbs she often positioned herself to attract. She may achieve in death what she could not achieve in court: she may provide some

Diana's experience with the media led her to campaign for privacy rights.

understanding of the universal need for a right to be let alone.

If her death produces the law she failed to create in life, she will have the last laugh; or, as the papers would have put it, the last infectious giggle.[150]

Another of Diana's legacies is that she brought renewed attention to the question of the future of the British monarchy. After her death, Prime Minister Tony Blair sensed that Britons shared Diana's belief that change was needed in the monarchy, to make it less distant from the people and more caring. Commenting on the queen's televised eulogy for Diana, Blair said, "Something must come of all this."[151]

Some said there was no doubt about it: Diana had changed England's monarchy forever. According to monarchy historian David Starkey, "That monarchy [before Diana] is over. It's dead, and on its tombstone will be written: Died at the hands of Diana, Princess of Wales, 1997."[152]

Author Salman Rushdie wrote after her death that Diana seemed far happier once she had escaped from the royal family. He suggested that perhaps Britain itself would be happier if it made the same escape and learned to live without kings and queens.

Diana also left behind a legacy of caring for the sick and less privileged. After her death, donations poured in so rapidly to the Diana, Princess of Wales, Memorial Fund for her favorite charities that officials estimated the total to reach $1 billion or more.

But more than raising money for charities, Diana left a sense of caring for others that she transferred to her sons. It was as if

It was Diana's hope that Princes William (left) and Harry (right) would share her concern for the needs of those less fortunate.

she wanted everyone to be part of one worldwide, loving family. To express this, she once said, "I always feed my children love and affection. It's so important." [153]

"She had a huge capacity for unhappiness, which is why she responded so well to the suffering of humanity," [154] Diana's close friend Lady Rosa Monckton explained. It helped explain why so many people responded to the legacy of her humanity.

The outpouring of grief and overwhelming number of flower bouquets and other sentiments that followed Diana's death left no question that she was beloved of the people. A note scrawled on a pink ballet slipper by a mourner and tied to the gates of Kensington Palace, where Diana had lived, summed up her fairy tale–like life: "You were a Cinderella at the Ball, and now you are a Sleeping Beauty." [155]

Diana's greatest legacy may well be her place in people's hearts. There, she would remain a princess forever.

Notes

Introduction: Princess and Humanitarian

1. Andrew Morton, *Diana: Her True Story.* New York: Simon & Schuster, 1997, pp. 282–83.

Chapter 1: The Girlhood of a Princess

2. Quoted in Nicholas Davies, *Diana: A Princess and Her Troubled Marriage.* New York: Birch Lane/Carol, 1992, p. 30.
3. Quoted in Morton, *Diana: Her True Story,* p. 23.
4. Quoted in Donald Spoto, *Diana: The Last Year.* New York: Harmony/Crown, 1997, p. 41.
5. Quoted in Morton, *Diana: Her True Story,* p. 23.
6. Quoted in Morton, *Diana: Her True Story,* p. 25.
7. Quoted in Morton, *Diana: Her True Story,* p. 26.
8. Quoted in Anthony Holden, *Diana: Her Life and Her Legacy.* New York: Random House, 1997, p. 32.
9. Quoted in Morton, *Diana: Her True Story,* p. 24.
10. Quoted in Morton, *Diana: Her True Story,* p. 28.
11. Quoted in Sean R. Pollock, ed., *Newsmakers 1997.* Detroit: Gale, 1997, p. 117.
12. Quoted in A & E Television Networks, *Biography,* "Diana: Her True Story," part 1, April 22, 1999.
13. Quoted in Ingrid Seward, *Diana: An Intimate Portrait.* Chicago: Contemporary Books, 1988, p. 35.
14. Quoted in Morton, *Diana: Her True Story,* p. 31.
15. Quoted in Penny Junor, *Diana, Princess of Wales.* Garden City, NY: Doubleday, 1983, p. 90.
16. Quoted in A & E Television Networks, *Biography,* "Diana," part 1.

17. Quoted in A & E Television Networks, *Biography,* "Diana, part 1.
18. Quoted in Morton, *Diana: Her True Story,* p. 94.

Chapter 2: A Royal Courtship and Marriage

19. Quoted in Morton, *Diana: Her True Story,* p. 126.
20. Quoted in Morton, *Diana: Her True Story,* p. 110.
21. Quoted in Pollock, *Newsmakers 1997,* p. 117.
22. Lady Colin Campbell, *Diana in Private,* p. 81.
23. Quoted in Morton, *Diana: Her True Story,* p. 112.
24. Quoted in Morton, *Diana: Her True Story,* p. 116.
25. Quoted in Robert Lacey, *Princess.* New York: Times Books, 1982, p. 18.
26. Quoted in Lacey, *Princess,* p. 18.
27. Quoted in Lacey, *Princess,* p. 18.
28 Quoted in Spoto, *Diana,* p. 58.
29. Quoted in Spoto, *Diana,* p. 58.
30. Quoted in Morton, *Diana: Her True Story,* p. 120.
31. Quoted in Lacey, *Princess,* p. 23.
32. Quoted in Morton, *Diana: Her True Story,* p. 125.
33. Quoted in Morton, *Diana: Her True Story,* p. 125.
34. Quoted in Gordon Carr, producer, *Diana: A Celebration, the People's Princess.* BBC Television Video, New York: Twayne Publishers, 1997.
35. Quoted in Lacey, *Princess,* p. 28.
36. Quoted in Lacey, *Princess,* p. 27.

Chapter 3: The Public Princess

37. Quoted in Penny Junor, *Charles: Victim or Villain?* New York: HarperCollins, 1998, p. 114.
38. Quoted in Christopher Andersen, *The Day Diana Died.* New York: Random House, 1998, p. 39.
39. Quoted in Morton, *Diana: Her True Story,* p. 47.
40. Quoted in Morton, *Diana: Her True Story,* p. 67.
41. Quoted in Morton, *Diana: Her True Story,* p. 35.
42. Quoted in *People Weekly,* "Too Close for Comfort," September 15, 1997, p. 71.
43. Quoted in Pollock, *Newsmakers 1997,* p. 119.

44. Quoted in Davies, *Diana,* p. 177.

45. Junor, *Charles,* p. 149.

46. Quoted in Martha Duffy, "A Royal Star Shines on Her Own," *Time,* July 29, 1991, p. 64.

47. Quoted in Michelle Green, "Queen of Hearts," *People Weekly,* September 15, 1997, p. 73.

48. Quoted in Morton, *Diana: Her True Story,* pp. 64–65.

49. Quoted in Morton, *Diana: Her True Story,* p. 245.

50. Quoted in Green, "Queen of Hearts," p. 73.

51. Quoted in Duffy, "A Royal Star Shines On Her Own," p. 64.

52. Quoted in Andrew Morton, *Diana: Her New Life.* New York: Simon & Schuster, 1994, p. 96.

53. Quoted in Morton, *Diana: Her True Story,* p. 167.

54. Quoted in Morton, *Diana: Her True Story,* p. 172.

55. Jonathan Dimbleby, *The Prince of Wales.* New York: Morrow, 1994, pp. 485–86.

56. Quoted in Dimbleby, *The Prince of Wales,* p. 488.

Chapter 4: The Private Princess

57. Quoted in Morton, *Diana: Her True Story,* p. 57.

58. Quoted in Morton, *Diana: Her True Story,* p. 48.

59. Quoted in Morton, *Diana: Her True Story,* pp. 46–47.

60. Quoted in Davies, *Diana,* p. 126.

61. Quoted in Spoto, *Diana,* p. 87.

62. Quoted in Spoto, *Diana,* p. 87.

63. Quoted in Davies, *Diana,* p. 126.

64. Quoted in A & E Television Networks, *Biography,* "Diana," part 1.

65. Quoted in Morton, *Diana: Her True Story,* p. 65.

66. Quoted in Holden, *Diana,* p. 52.

67. Quoted in ABC Television News, *Diana: Legacy of a Princess, 1961–1997.* MPI Home Video, 1997.

68. Quoted in Morton, *Diana: Her True Story,* p. 35.

69. Quoted in Morton, *Diana: Her True Story,* p. 39.

70. Quoted in Morton, *Diana: Her True Story,* p. 39.

71. Quoted in Morton, *Diana: Her True Story,* pp. 41–42.

72. Quoted in Morton, *Diana: Her True Story,* p. 42.

73. Quoted in Morton, *Diana: Her True Story,* p. 39.

74. Quoted in Morton, *Diana: Her True Story,* p. 37.
75. Quoted in Howard Chua-Eoan, "In Living Memory," *Time,* September 15, 1997, p. 73
76. Quoted in Spoto, *Diana,* p. 102.
77. Quoted in Morton, *Diana: Her True Story,* p. 56.
78. Quoted in Morton, *Diana: Her True Story,* p. 41.
79. Quoted in Morton, *Diana: Her True Story,* p. 41.
80. Quoted in Morton, *Diana: Her True Story,* p. 42.
81. Quoted in Morton, *Diana: Her True Story,* pp. 42–43.
82. Quoted in Morton, *Diana: Her True Story,* p. 56.
83. Quoted in Morton, *Diana: Her True Story,* p. 51.
84. Quoted in Morton, *Diana: Her True Story,* pp. 51–52.
85. Junor, *Charles,* p. 127.
86. Quoted in Pollock, *Newsmakers 1997,* p. 119.

Chapter 5: The End of a Fairy Tale

87. Quoted in Sally Bedell Smith, *Diana in Search of Herself.* New York: Times Books, 1999, p. 218.
88. Quoted in A & E Television Networks, *Biography,* "Diana," part 2.
89. Quoted in Davies, *Diana,* p. 25.
90. Junor, *Charles,* p. 96.
91. Pollock, *Newsmakers 1997,* p. 119.
92. Quoted in Morton, *Diana: Her True Story,* p. 61.
93. Quoted in Anderson, *The Day Diana Died,* pp. 47–48.
94. Quoted in Morton, *Diana: Her New Life,* p. 30.
95. Quoted in Smith, *Diana in Search of Herself,* p. 264.
96. Quoted in Smith, *Diana in Search of Herself,* p. 264.
97. Quoted in Smith, *Diana in Search of Herself,* p. 264.
98. Quoted in Smith, *Diana in Search of Herself,* p. 264.
99. Quoted in Chua-Eoan, "In Living Memory," p. 73
100. Quoted in Smith, *Diana in Search of Herself,* p. 264.
101. Quoted in Seward, *Diana,* p. 8.
102. Quoted in Chua-Eoan, "In Living Memory," p. 73.
103. Quoted in Joe Chidley, "The Tabloid Princess," *Maclean's,* September 8, 1997, p. 36.
104. Quoted in BBC, *Panorama,* Princess Diana television interview, November 20, 1995.

105. Quoted in BBC, *Panorama,* Princess Diana television interview.

106. Quoted in BBC, *Panorama,* Princess Diana television interview.

107. Quoted in Andersen, *The Day Diana Died,* p. 56.

108. Junor, *Charles,* pp. 288–89.

109. Junor, *Charles,* p. 163.

110. Quoted in Spoto, *Diana,* p. 96.

Chapter 6: The People's Princess

111. Quoted in A & E Television Networks, *Biography,* "Diana," part 2.

112. Quoted in Spoto, *Diana,* p. 119.

113. Quoted in Spoto, *Diana,* p. 152.

114. Quoted in Spoto, *Diana,* p. 60.

115. Quoted in CNN, "Princess Diana," *People Profiles,* May 27, 1999.

116. Quoted in Spoto, *Diana,* p. 147.

117. Quoted in Morton, *Diana: Her New Life,* p. 104.

118. Quoted in Morton, *Diana: Her New Life,* p. 104.

119. Quoted in Spoto, *Diana,* p. 96.

120. Quoted in ABC Television News, *Diana.*

121. Quoted in Andersen, *The Day Diana Died,* p. 58.

122. Quoted in D'Arcy Jenish, "The Lady with a Cause," *Maclean's,* September 15, 1997, p. 55.

123. Quoted in Spoto, *Diana,* p. 132.

124. Quoted in A & E Television Networks, *Biography,* "Diana," part 2.

125. Quoted in Nomi Morris, "A Jet-Setting Don Juan," *Maclean's,* September 15, 1997, p. 54.

126. Quoted in Morris, "A Jet-Setting Don Juan," p. 54.

127. Quoted in Spoto, *Diana,* p. 65.

128. Quoted in A & E Television Networks, *Biography,* "Diana," part 2.

129. Quoted in Smith, *Diana in Search of Herself,* p. 348.

130. Quoted in Morton, *Diana: Her True Story,* p. 273.

131. Quoted in Morton, *Diana: Her True Story,* p. 275.

132. Quoted in Morton, *Diana: Her True Story,* p. 275.

133. Richard Kay, "My Talk with Diana the Day She Died," *McCall's*, December 1997, p. 40.
134. Kay, "My Talk with Diana the Day She Died," p. 44.
135. Quoted in Spoto, *Diana,* p. 181.
136. Quoted in Barbara Kantrowitz, "Princess of the World," *Newsweek,* December 22, 1997, p. 62.
137. Quoted in Kantrowitz, "Princess of the World," p. 62.
138. Quoted in Andersen, *The Day Diana Died,* pp. 260–61.
139. Quoted in Spoto, *Diana,* p. 24.

Epilogue: The Enigmatic Princess

140. Smith, *Diana in Search of Herself,* p. 360.
141. Quoted in Smith, *Diana in Search of Herself,* p. 360.
142. Quoted in Smith, *Diana in Search of Herself,* p. 360.
143. Quoted in Smith, *Diana in Search of Herself,* p. 361.
144. Smith, *Diana in Search of Herself,* p. 361.
145. Smith, *Diana in Search of Herself,* p. 363.
146. Smith, *Diana in Search of Herself,* p. 365.
147. Dimbleby, *The Prince of Wales,* p. 393.
148. Smith, *Diana in Search of Herself,* p. 368.
149. Smith, *Diana in Search of Herself,* p. 7.
150. Geoffrey Robertson, "Privacy Matters," *New Yorker,* September 15, 1997, pp. 38–40.
151. Quoted in Holden, *Diana,* p. 15.
152. Quoted in ABC Television News, *Diana.*
153. Quoted in Sam Helliker, "How the Princess Lives On," *McCall's,* December 1997, p. 48.
154. Quoted in Helliker, "How the Princess Lives On," p. 48.
155. Quoted in Barry Hillenbrand, "Farewell, Diana," *Time,* September 16, 1997, p. 40.

Important Dates in the Life of Princess Diana

1961

Born the Honorable Diana Spencer on July 1 to Viscount Althorp (Edward John Spencer) and Lady Frances Ruth Burke Roche Spencer.

1969

Parents divorce; she is placed in the custody of her father.

1977

Meets Charles, Prince of Wales, through her sister Sarah.

1981

Becomes engaged to Prince Charles on February 24; they marry on July 29.

1982

Prince William is born on June 21.

1984

Prince Henry is born on September 15.

1986

Rumors of bulimia begin; marital troubles are noticed by the media.

1992

Andrew Morton's book *Diana: Her True Story* is published in June; Prime Minister John Major announces Diana and Charles's separation.

1993

Delivers "Time and Space" speech on December 3, announcing retirement from public life.

1994

Prince Charles gives televised interview on June 29 admitting to adultery.

1995

Gives first solo television interview on BBC's *Panorama,* admitting to an affair with James Hewitt.

1996

Divorce from Prince Charles is finalized on August 28.

1997

Visits land-mine victims in Angola and Bosnia; donates gowns to charity; dies in Paris automobile accident with companion Dodi Fayed on August 31; is buried on September 6 at Althorp estate.

For Further Reading

Kristine Brennan, *Diana, Princess of Wales*. Philadelphia: Chelsea House, 1999. A young-adult biography of Diana.

Marc Cerasini, *Diana: Queen of Hearts*. New York: Random House, 1997. The life and death of Diana, for middle-school readers.

Michael O'Mara, ed., *Diana, Princess of Wales: A Tribute in Photographs*. New York: St. Martin's, 1997. An illustrated biography of Diana; although this is an adult book, it is appropriate for younger readers.

Henry Rasof, *Picture Life of Charles and Diana*. New York: Franklin Watts, 1988. A young-adult illustrated book on the married life of the Prince and Princess of Wales.

Thomas Sancton and Scott MacLeod, *Death of a Princess—the Investigation*. New York: St. Martin's, 1998. A report on the causes of the auto accident in which Princess Diana died; an adult book suitable for young adults.

Websites

Britannia (www.britannia.com/diana/). This website has links to information about Diana's life and death in "A Remembrance of Princess Diana."

The British Monarchy: The Official Web Site (www.royal.gov.uk/start.htm). In addition to providing information about the monarchy and its history, this site also contains a biography of the late Princess of Wales.

CNN.com (www.cnn.com/WORLD/9708/diana/). This site features an in-depth report on the circumstances surrounding Princess Diana's death entitled "The Death of Princess Diana."

Diana, Princess of Wales, Memorial Fund (www.thework
continues.org). This website describes how Diana's charitable works are continuing after her death.

Princess Diana Videos and CDs (www.geocities.com/
Athens/Aegean/7545/Diana2.html). A list of videos and
compact disc recordings about Princess Diana can be found
on this website.

Works Consulted

Books

Christopher Andersen, *The Day Diana Died*. New York: Random House, 1998. A detailed report on events leading up to the death of Princess Diana. This adult book is appropriate for young-adult readers.

Lady Colin Campbell, *Diana in Private: The Princess Nobody Knows*. New York: St. Martin's, 1992. A book about events in Diana's life that led to her separation from Prince Charles.

Nicholas Davies, *Diana: A Princess and Her Troubled Marriage*. New York: Birch Lane/Carol, 1992. A biography of Princess Diana up to the last five years of her life; an adult book suitable for young adults.

Jonathan Dimbleby, *The Prince of Wales*. New York: Morrow, 1994. An adult biography of Prince Charles that is also suitable for young adults.

Anthony Holden, *Charles at Fifty*. New York: Random House, 1998. An adult biography of Prince Charles suitable for young adults.

——, *Diana: Her Life and Her Legacy*. New York: Random House, 1997. A picture book with text about Diana's life and her impact on the public and on the British monarchy; an adult book suitable for young-adult readers.

Penny Junor, *Charles: Victim or Villain?* New York: HarperCollins, 1998. Adult book assessing Prince Charles's relationship with Princess Diana; suitable for young-adult readers.

——, *Diana, Princess of Wales*. Garden City, NY: Doubleday,

1983. This book covers the early years and social work of Princess Diana; an adult book suitable for young adults.

Robert Lacey, *Princess.* New York: Times Books, 1982. A well-illustrated biography of Diana and her first year as the Princess of Wales.

Andrew Morton, *Diana: Her New Life.* New York: Simon & Schuster, 1994. Diana after her divorce.

————, *Diana: Her True Story.* New York: Simon & Schuster, 1997. The book contains Diana's notes for this biography, titled "In Her Own Words." It is a comprehensive adult biography that is appropriate for young adults and tells of her life and death.

Sean R. Pollock, ed., *Newsmakers 1997.* Detroit: Gale, 1997. This book focuses on people who were in the news in 1997 and includes a short biography of Princess Diana.

Ingrid Seward, *Diana: An Intimate Portrait.* Chicago: Contemporary Books, 1988. An adult book about Diana's life and humanitarian work preceding her separation and divorce from Prince Charles. It is suitable for young adults.

Sally Bedell Smith, *Diana in Search of Herself.* New York: Times Books, 1999. The life of Princess Diana from a psychological and mental-health approach. Suitable for young-adult readers.

Donald Spoto, *Diana: The Last Year.* New York: Harmony/ Crown, 1997. A biography of Diana focusing on events leading up to her death and analyzing the accident that caused it.

Periodicals

Joe Chidley, "The Tabloid Princess," *Maclean's,* September 8, 1997.

Howard Chua-Eoan, "In Living Memory," *Time,* September 15, 1997.

Martha Duffy, "A Royal Star Shines on Her Own," *Time,* July 29, 1991.

Michelle Green, "Queen of Hearts," *People Weekly,* September 15, 1997.

Sam Helliker, "How the Princess Lives On," *McCall's,* December 1997.

Barry Hillenbrand, "Farewell, Diana," *Time,* September 16, 1997.

D'Arcy Jenish, "The Lady with a Cause," *Maclean's,* September 15, 1997.

Barbara Kantrowitz, "Princess of the World," *Newsweek,* December 22, 1997.

Richard Kay, "My Talk with Diana the Day She Died," *McCall's,* December 1997.

Nomi Morris, "A Jet-Setting Don Juan," *Maclean's,* September 15, 1997.

People Weekly, "Too Close for Comfort," September 15, 1997.

Geoffrey Robertson, "Privacy Matters," *New Yorker,* September 15, 1997.

Salman Rushdie, "Crash," *New Yorker,* September 15, 1997.

Television and Video Sources

ABC Television News, *Diana: Legacy of a Princess, 1961–1997.* New York: MPI Home Video, 1997. A documentary on the life and death of Diana.

A & E Television Networks, New York: *Biography,* "Diana: Her True Story," April 22 and 23, 1999. A two-part television program with movie clips and interviews with and about Princess Diana.

A & E Television Networks, New York: *Biography,* "Prince Charles," June 24, 1994. A television program with movie clips and interviews with and about Prince Charles.

BBC, *Panorama,* Princess Diana television interview, November 20, 1995. The only television interview Diana granted, which caused a sensation.

CNN, Cable News Network, New York: Princess Diana, People Profiles, May 27, 1999.

Gordon Carr, producer, *Diana: A Celebration, the People's Princess.* BBC Television Video, New York: Twayne Publishers, 1997. A video tribute to the life of Princess Diana.

Index

Picture Credits

About the Author

Walter Oleksy writes novels and nonfiction books for preteens, young adults, and adults.

His novels include *If I'm Lost, How Come I Found You?; Bug Scanner and the Computer Mystery; Land of the Lost Dinosaurs;* and *The Pirates of Deadman's Cay.*

His nonfiction books include *The Information Revolution, Hispanic-American Scientists, The Philippines, Mikhail Gorbachev; A Leader for Soviet Change, The Black Plague,* and *Careers in the Animal Kingdom.*

Oleksy lives in a Chicago suburb with his dog Max, a black lab-shepherd mix who loves to swim and fetch tennis balls.